Love and Death in Rhodes

OTHER NOVELS BY MARCIA FINE

Historical Fiction

Hidden Ones—A Veil of Memories

Paper Children—An Immigrant's Legacy

The Blind Eye—A Sephardic Journey

Paris Lamb

Satire

Stressed In Scottsdale

Boomerang—When Life Comes Back To Bite You

Gossip.com

Love and Death in Rhodes

MARCIA FINE

L'IMAGE PRESS

Published by Limage Press

Historical Fiction | Sephardic Jews | Rhodes | Holocaust | Kahal Shalom Synagogue | Women's Fiction | Italians WWII

ISBN Paperback: 978-0-9826952-9-6
ISBN eBook: 978-0-9986845-1-2

Poem "I only wanted to write about them": Swan Isle Press, *The White Islands / Las Islas Blancas.* © by Marjorie Agosín; translation © by Jacqueline Nafito.

Printed in the United States of America

For the Rhodeslis who did not return

I only wanted to write about them

I only wanted to write about them,

Narrate their fierce audacity,

Their voyages through the channels of the Mediterranean.

With their prayer book laminated in gold.

I only wanted to speak about them as if everything were

   touched by the gesture of love.

To speak about the Sephardim

Who traveled with poppies in their hair

Travelers with flowery languages, from one island to another, From one corner of the world to another.

Amidst the whispers

Only a song,

The voice that remembers.

The tenacious voice of an undeniable faith.

"Any European power who was master of Rhodes would at once hold the key of the Archipelago, of Greece, of Smyrna, of the Dardanelles, and the Seas of Egypt and Syria. I do not know in the world a better maritime military position, a finer climate, or a more prolific soil."

—Alphonse de Lamartine,
1832 upon visiting Rhodes

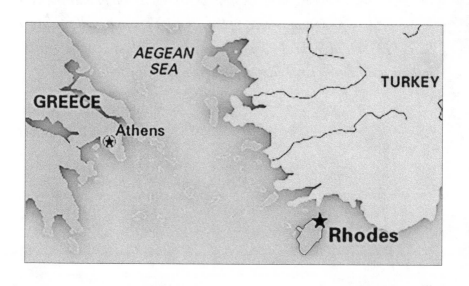

Preface

The ocean receded and swelled, waves spraying the bronzed children as they initiated games near the blue-green water, splashing into the surf. As a fading sun illuminated the trees into whipped flames, the young Rhodeslis heard their parents yelling a cacophony of names from the street as they whooped and skipped toward their waiting families. They regretted abandoning the last breaths of daylight freedom. Luna, the tallest and a leader among the girls, knows she is too old for them. She wants to remain a child as long as possible but her body does not lie. Her chest has grown, despite her mother's white binding cloth.

Feisty in attitude yet demure with her family, she takes in the salty air with closed eyes. She taps the mezuzah, its prayers wrapped tight inside, on the right side of the door of her parents' modest home, passes her fingers to her lips and lowers her head to enter. Her mother acknowledges her with a nod toward the faucet to urge a hand-washing as she stirs eggplants, squash and tomatoes with cumin and pine nuts in a frying pan. The aroma of olive oil, garlic and vegetables teases Luna. Her mother states, "You are too old to play with children anymore." She leaves her wooden spoon on the stove to hold Luna's face in her hands, their coffee-colored eyes searching the other. "Besides, it is the Sabbath, *mi ija*."

BOOK ONE

Luna

Chapter One

1935

The first time I saw him he marched down the street near our home with his battalion. He wore the pressed blue uniforms of the Italian navy. He was taller than most on the island, broad shouldered and stiff with the pride of his regiment.

I stretched to my full height while my friends giggled behind me. The Italians had been on our island of paradise since 1911. When Mussolini sent more troops in the 1930s, we weren't alarmed. It was a friendly occupation, if there is such a thing. Our cultures mutually embraced family, food and *joie de vivre*, a phrase I learned in my French class.

The next time I saw him we were gathered at the end of Market Street near the fountain. We didn't need chaperones like other Jewish girls who lived on the mainland. Our island afforded us some modicum of independence.

My mother and I attended Kahal Shalom synagogue for some Shabbat services and holidays. We sat in the *azara* with the other women, away from my father and older brothers. I loved the translation of the name: Holy Congregation of Peace. As a young child, when I was learning the history of Rhodes, the Rabbi taught me that our house of worship was built in 1577. The Jews had a presence on our island for 2300 years! We sat near the south wall, peeking at the sanctuary through curtains, as the *shofar*, a ram's horn, was sounded as a warning to Jews to awaken and improve their ways. We covered our eyes as Moses had because the poignant sound was supposed to be the voice of G-d. My mother, anxious to return home to complete our supper, bowed her head.

Later, when I ran to the market for an onion my mother needed and that our neighbors didn't have, I saw him sitting with other officers at a café. I hurried. Men, in general, especially those of another faith were not part of my world. I was promised to a son in the Aldaheff family when I turned fifteen. Or maybe sixteen. My father liked having me around because I was a good, curious student, unlike my brothers. They were only interested in what they needed from our Hebrew texts. I could sit for hours going over *parshas* with him, whereas my older brothers, their minds wandered to what was outside the thick plastered walls of our home.

With my waist-length hair rolled under a scarf as was customary for women of our faith, I barely glanced at him. Yet, we were both aware of each other.

The Italians on our island were not received with hostility as occupiers, but as a compliment to our culture. We adored their cuisine, (a word my friend taught me after she traveled in Europe with her family) and culture—with a rich history like ours with slaves and kings, their operas, although the rabbi didn't approve of the racy plots—even though I heard him humming the theme of *Tosca* when I stood near him in the market. The terrible defeat in 70 AD of the Jews by the Emperor Vespasian and his son, Titus, from Rome was a story my father repeated so we understood the gravity of defeat. "Someday we will walk underneath the Arch of Titus in Rome that the father erected to honor his son after capturing thirty thousand Jewish slaves, all to prove we are still here," was my father's wish.

We had a lot in common with the Italians who influenced our lives in many ways. They loved life, never dour, always singing, playing instruments, guitars pressed into a soldier's hand with melodies that drifted to my home as our open windows searched for breezes. Their culinary pleasure of fresh glazed pasta glistened with oil, garlic, fresh tomatoes and oregano from our gardens. They adored our abundance of fruits and vegetables as much as we did—peaches, mandarins, grapes, melons, plums, olives, eggplants, cucumbers, zucchini, garlic, onion, tomatoes and potatoes. They were all eaten the day they were picked from small farms on the western side of the island or our own backyards. My mother raised dill and mint on our kitchen windowsill that she traded for other spices with neighbors.

Although we studied Italian in school, the girls separated from the boys, of course, our instructor wasn't fluent. When he spoke it was halted, not the mellifluous sounds that floated between two Italians, their expressions and hand gestures making communication a dance flowing in the ocean breezes.

Mussolini wanted us all to speak Italian. No more Greek and their Orthodox Church. We were delighted. The Italians were more compassionate than the Greeks. My father called the Greeks barbaric after they cut down the peach trees on our island for firewood. Why destroy what we could all share?

In the year 1929 our idyllic island did not feel the impact of a world-wide financial crash, other than exports piled up at the docks, so we had plenty to eat. Mothers would go to the waiting ships and bargain for the best vegetables and fruit scheduled to leave the island, haggling with the ship captain over fruit ready to rot, gnats making petite black clouds.

On one of our market trips to Calle Ancha, when my mother and I, baskets over our arms, heads turned to pick the best of what was offered, the tall Italian came over to introduce himself. "Signore Luigi di Liscia at your service." I cast my eyes downward, noticing that his leather laced boots were the same as the soldiers who marched around the island. My mother did her best not to engage, but he was charming, eyes crinkly when he smiled, his teeth white perfection.

"I'm a lonely young man of nineteen far from my beloved Roma. I've never been to an island as this. Would it be possible to have your daughter familiarize me with the local customs?"

With my upward squint I saw the horror on my mother's face.

"Oh, no. I am sorry. My daughter cannot do such a thing," her voice filled with fear. She pulled the knot on her shawl tighter. Young women were protected in our society. Besides, I was promised, as were most of my friends. Old customs were still in place in the new century.

"Perhaps I can explain myself better. I do not mean to frighten you. I'm a soldier far from home. I play guitar," he offered to placate any insults.

"Captain." My mother's voice was firm. Didn't he know she had dismissed him?

"I am a mere *tecnico di macchina* in the Reggia Marina,"

"Sorry, Signore, but our daughters cannot keep company with young men."

He looked surprised. "But I am a machinist's mate, a mere sailor." A look of knowing passed across his face. "Of course. I meant no harm. May I ask your name and your daughter's?"

"I am Signora Carmela and this is my daughter, Eleanora."

"I go by Luna," I said, lifting my head for the first time to stare at him. His black hair was cut short, his teeth were straight, something my grandmother admired in others and his coffee eyes warmed my face as I felt pink rise to my cheeks. I looked away.

Weeks later, after we had crossed paths more than a few times, I saw him near the fountain with the two sea horses at the main square. It was late in the day and I was there with my friends while our mothers shared *platicos*, plates of candies and baked goods, for the upcoming Sabbath. We all stared at him as he perched on the edge of the fountain and played an Italian song for us on his guitar. We were smitten. Joya, who sometimes called herself by the Italian version, Gioia, sighed and leaned into me, "Play your mandolin for him."

He heard her and addressed me directly, "Perhaps you can bring your instrument and we can make music together."

"No. Th-That would not be allowed," I stammered.

"Why not?"

"Because we are Jews of the Sephardic culture."

He stepped back, surprised. "You are all Jews?"

We nodded in unison as my mother returned to my side. "Not you again," she said in a half-hearted way.

"Yes, Signora. I learned your daughter plays the mandolin."

"Yes, true. But she will not play for you," she said as she pulled her shoulders back.

"Why not?" His amiability seemed frozen.

"Because she is betrothed to the Aldaheff boy since she was twelve."

His eyebrows rose. If that did not have enough impact, she added, "She's fifteen. That's late for our community The wedding is planned for next year."

The girls had teased me about my "Italian soldier" It was apparent he was very interested in me. His mouth turned downward as he sucked his bottom lip in palpable disappointment.

My mother wrapped her shawl tight around her shoulders and picked up our plate of sweets from the other women. "Come, mi ija, it is time to prepare for supper."

I gave a small wave to the group as I trailed my mother through the byzantine alleys to our home. Bright pink and orange bougainvillea draped the doorway, colorful leaves tickling in the breeze.

I was flattered by the attention. I knew it was not G-d's choice for me to feel such things. It was forbidden to interact with the population outside of our *erub* community, a line defined by sages and rabbis. Yet, my mind went to the Italian— a navy man, and not to the pale Alhadeff boy who spent hours studying the Torah.

The next day, Joya found me with my watering can in our small courtyard, my hair wrapped in one of my mother's old scarves. I wetted down the diosmose, bursting with pink flowers, thymari and rigani, known as thyme and oregano, according to my dictionary translation, that bloomed in abundance.

"Do you want to know what happened after you and your mother left yesterday?" she teased, shifting from foot to foot.

I pretended disinterest as my can splashed water near the roots of the pink and white bougainvillea that climbed our front courtyard wall, along with purple lavender and yellow laurel. "The Italian wanted to know more about you." She smirked at me. I felt guilty without doing a thing other than saying my name.

"What did he say?" I wanted to forget his wavy hair and uniform. Italians were like us—singers, dancers, lovers of good food and wine. We appreciated life. Ceremonial wine was considered a gift from G-d, although my brothers imbibed with raki, a Turkish liqueur.

"He wanted to know why you were betrothed so young."

9

"What did you say?"

"I told him we were of the Jewish faith, Sephardim specifically." She crossed her arms across her chest with authority.

"And?" I wanted to shake the truth from her lips.

"He stood straighter and said, "It's of no matter to me. I want to know the young woman, Luna. She's like the moon, evasive, far away, watching me through clouds." We giggled.

"I shook my head from side to side. Finally, with the rest of our friends urging me, I explained that there was little intermarriage on the island. I added, "Besides, Luna is promised.""

Chapter Two

It was only a matter of time before he showed up at our door on a lazy Sunday afternoon. My father, who had returned from his travels buying and selling notions on the mainland before the Sabbath, was stern when he saw a navy man. The Italian removed his hat. I was hiding in the archway to our sleeping quarters.

My father introduced himself in a formal manner. "I am Isaac Avzaradel. How may I help you?" He did not extend his hand.

After the Italian introduced himself as Luigi Quorino di Liscia, he beseeched my father in Italian. My father understood him as he used the language for business along with Greek, Turkish and smatterings of French and English. "Perhaps I can play some music for you and your family." My father's hand began to shut the door.

"Wait. I miss my family. Yes, I am a Catholic, but not so religious that I go to church or affiliate with the Greek Orthodox. I am looking for solace from the nearby military base."

In an instant his guitar flipped from his back to his front and he strummed a familiar Italian song I knew called "Lolita." My father

11

must have been captivated too, because he did not stop him. My mother peeked over my father's shoulder entranced by the music and his sweet voice.

I turned toward my room, grabbed my mandolin from the corner of the white-washed walls and, out of sight, I plucked the melody and hummed the tune. It was a serenade from the angels. My parents and I were transfixed. When it ended, my father invited him into our living space. I was shocked at his hospitality, which we only offered to others in our community. Little did I realize that my father had opened the door to so much more.

In Ladino my mother hissed at my father, "What are you doing? He is sweet on Luna."

"Never mind. I like the music. It cannot hurt for us to have an ally in the Italian navy. Make a glass of tea. She is promised anyway."

My mother was surprised. She returned to the kitchen in the back of the house and admonished me to pick mint leaves from the herbs on our window sill.

Soon my brothers emerged from their torpor to investigate the commotion of the unknown guest. Their bodies filled our living space. More introductions. Never mind the guitar. Do you have a gun? I carried in a tray of glasses, a sprig of fresh mint leaf decorating the lip of each one.

I remained quiet watching the camaraderie unfold between the men about San Angelo del Pesco, where his family lived in a small village in the mountains. My father asked, "What do you do when not serving your country?"

"Teaching is my profession, although my family would like me to assist with the land. I also play music with a group to celebrate weddings," Luigi smiled.

He seemed a happy young man, content with his lot in life. I was curious as to what he taught and to whom, but it was not my place to ask. At that moment, my older brother, Bohor, began to gasp for air holding his chest. It happened often where he could not grab a breath, a fish floundering on the dock for air. He collapsed on the rug as my parents rushed to him. The soldier knelt and bent over him too. Coughs racked his body. My father pulled him close in a hug to calm him. It did not stop the tortured sounds he was making as he wheezed in and out.

The Italian spoke in a soft voice. "Do you have ephedra leaves? They usually grow near the shore."

We all seemed puzzled.

"When you pulverize them in red wine, it usually stops this."

"How do you know?" my mother questioned as my brother continued to open his mouth to grasp for air, his lips curled outward.

"My *nonnina* had this. It won't cure it, but it calms one down so he can breathe normally. Do you have any?"

"No. We have no such thing."

I was worried. My parents had lost another sibling as a baby years ago to this same malady.

I spoke out, "I know where it grows near the water's edge."

"Run," the Italian told me. "Bring back leaves."

"Hurry!" My father held Bohor's body tight against his chest. "Rodolfo, go with her."

My brother and I pulled on our gardening shoes and we ran. It was less than fifteen minutes before we returned. Bohor, his clothes disheveled, was sitting on the sofa smiling when we rushed in, breathless as when we left him.

The Italian explained to my parents, "When Pliny the Elder wrote about natural remedies he focused on respiratory issues he thought were enhanced by pollen and dust. Pulverized ephedra leaves added to red wine works for many."

I held out my hand, after dipping it into my apron and displayed the leaves.

"Yes, that's them," he confirmed. "Save them in a glass jar in a cool place. Fresh are best, but it is helpful to always have some available. Do you keep wine in your home?"

My father bristled. "For ceremonial purposes only." His intention was to let this Gentile know we were not drinkers. Jews did not imbibe except on Purim where it was part of the holiday or on the Sabbath with prayers.

Bohor sipped the mixture my mother concocted as he leaned back into pillows on the sofa. He waved a hand to let the Italian know he was alright.

"It's getting late," the soldier announced as he stood. "I must get back to the base."

"How did you get here?" I inquired.

"A reliable bicycle," he said, as he slung his guitar across his back.

My father stood and saw him to the door. They shook hands. "Thank you, Signore, for your hospitality. I hope your son feels better." Then he looked back at me as I lowered my eyes.

Chapter Three

We didn't see the Italians for days because of maneuvers. Yet, this stranger inserted himself into our lives. An unexpected bottle of Italian wine was left at our door with a ribbon tied around its neck.

"We cannot drink wine that is not kosher!" my father fumed as he brought it inside.

"Why not?" my brothers Bohor and Rodolfo challenged.

"Because it breaks *kashrut* laws." I could hear the fury in my father's voice. "Throw it out."

"What difference would it make if we had a glass?" said Bohor.

"You would be breaking our kosher rules. It is not allowed."

"And you've never broken a law, especially when you travel and kosher food is not available?"

"No!" My father sounded like the roar of a large animal I once heard in the woods. "Are you accusing me?"

He and Bohor stood face-to-face. "Papa, I am not accusing you. I would like a taste. Maybe mamma could cook with it." Bohor backed down. My father's word was the law in our house.

"It is not possible." My father crossed his arms across his chest. These two agreed on little and had locked horns like angry goats.

Bohor changed the subject. "Where did it come from?"

My father's voice rose again. "Where do you think?" Bohor stared, confused. "The Italian who's sweet on your sister!" Bohor's mouth dropped open.

Such a thing was not acceptable in our community. I felt ashamed. I had done nothing to encourage him, knowing it was forbidden. My mother no longer allowed me to bind my breasts and gave me a contraption she insisted I wear every day. It pushed them out and up instead of squashing them flat. With the onset of menses they seemed to grow from oranges to grapefruits in a short span of time. My friends teased me that they were the largest on the island, a joke, of course.

Still, why had he left such a gift? Yes, I found his appearance appealing and the fact that he played guitar enchanting, but it was not allowed. I do not know what happened to the wine, but the argument permeated our home with a strained silence between my father and brother.

Then, without warning, our school closed without explanation. Later, I overheard my parents discussing the disappearance of the Headmaster and a few teachers. One left to assist family in Salonika, another joined his family bakery business and two more joined a merchant ship. Unusual circumstances, but the school was closed and my friends and I were left to find other activities to occupy our days.

At first, we were excited because of our freedom, but going to the market with our mothers was not teaching us anything. I loved learning, even though my father told me it was a waste.

"Women are meant to keep the house and raise the children," I was told on many occasions.

Later, after playing endless games with Joya and the others, I got bored. I missed learning Italian. It inspired me. It was a language of melodies, like the songs I strummed on my mandolin.

Signore di Liscia approached us as we idled near the fountain with the sea horses on a rare cloudy day.

"Why are you girls not in school?" he asked, glancing at me.

Joya told him about our closed school.

He sympathized. "What if I taught you Italian?"

We looked at each other with doubt. "Our parents would not allow such a thing," I answered. "Besides, where could we go?"

"Maybe the school will re-open when they find more teachers," offered Maria, the smallest among us and everyone's little sister.

"Perhaps if I taught all of you, your fathers and mothers would relent. Learning another language is important. Besides, as Italians we are here to stay. Mussolini plans to take over the world."

An avid campaign produced by ten young women convinced our families that speaking Italian was a good idea. Of course, I was the most vociferous and had the most opposition. My father and brothers thought it was a terrible idea, a threat to our Sephardic way of life. But, I was a brave girl and unrelenting when I wanted something.

"What is the reason we cannot learn when we have a willing teacher?" I challenged my mother. I thought if I could get her on my side she could convince my father that a young woman moping around the house was not worthwhile.

"Luna, you are betrothed to the Alhadeff boy. He comes from a good family. There's many on our island with that name. He's related through a distant cousin's marriage to the prominent ones who own two banks and the department store, although I don't think he's privy to their wealth. Enough. We are moving up the wedding. No more talk of Italian lessons."

My world came crashing down like an erupted volcano covering a rural village. Moving up the wedding? I had barely spoken to my intended. Had my parents collected all they needed for my dowry? I thought it would take another year! Besides, a dowry was supposed to be displayed for all to see. We hardly had anything ready except embroidered linens. I was not prepared to be anyone's wife, let alone to commit myself to cooking and cleaning for a man. I wanted to learn, but it appeared my education was over.

That is until I enlisted Joya and Maria to talk to their families. Not everyone thought learning Italian was so dangerous. I began a campaign to get the other parents to convince mine that this was a good idea. I gave a speech to the mothers first. I addressed them around the fountain.

"Dearest mothers of my friends, we are in the twentieth century. Times have changed. We are all good daughters of Sephardic Judaism. Let us not be idle. May we not pursue learning to enhance our lives? Italian, Greek, French are all languages we can teach our children when we are mothers. The world is expanding. So should our minds!" I implored with earnestness.

Eventually, the mothers told the fathers that it was a harmless venture that would benefit us and they relented. Except my parents, of course. They were adamant. It was not about learning Italian. Signore di Liscia was the problem. I begged and pleaded until finally, when my father was leaving for a trip to sell his notions on the other islands and visit his sister in Salonika, he relented. "Let her take the classes. I cannot bear the arguments of Luna any longer," he told my mother. As I walked into the living space where they were arguing, he commanded, "Go! Leave us alone with your crazy ideas. No more discussion. But, I will tell you that there cannot be any camaraderie with the Italian. He is a danger!"

Chapter Four

In a few weeks our class was formed, the Italian hired at a nominal fee and we sat in a classroom at the naval base. The younger girls giggled when we parked our bikes, Maria, the youngest, hanging onto my back. We had agreed to pay him a small amount in liras or drachmas per class. We felt awkward handing him coins so we bowed our heads and slipped them onto his desk.

At first we were properly behaved, but then Joya and I realized we could act up a bit because he would never tell our parents. We greeted Signore di Liscia with a loud "*boigorno*" in the morning and an "*arrevederchi*" as we flung our legs, skirts between our legs, over our bicycles. It was the highlight of our days learning proper greetings, simple sentences and vocabulary. There were no books, so we faced forward in rapt attention as he wrote phrases we were to memorize: *I am hungry, how do you feel, may I help*, on an old blackboard with a piece of chalk, the white dust powdering his hands. We whispered when he turned away from us, mostly in delight that we were as smart as foxes to convince our parents.

By the time my father had returned I was teaching my mother Italian phrases I deemed necessary like —*how much are your fruits and vegetables? Which way to the mountains from the ocean?* and *grazie* for thank you and *ciao* to say good-bye. My father dismissed us with an "Ach, you are wasting your time."

After a few weeks our teacher walked us to our bicycles parked outside the post. Soon he was a presence at the fountain with his guitar playing ballads or romantic tunes that wafted through our open windows.

"He's singing to you," said Joya. "He wants you."

I laughed off such sentiments, but inside I was drawn to this man. I did my best to push him out of my mind at night lying in my bed, embracing his angelic voice. Then I would catch myself, knowing that anything between us was forbidden. I was diligent with my prayers, saying the *Shema* over and over until sleep squeezed my eyes shut and my mind rolled over into an abyss.

It went on like that with me being the star student of the Italian language and harboring a fantasy of romantic notions. Then a tragedy struck our family. My father did not wake up one morning. My mother's wail alerted the entire household.

I will never know what happened, but Bohor and Rodolfo said he was clutching his chest. "It had to be his heart," they told me.

It was too late to call Doctor Cabrera. My poppa was gone. I clung to my mother while she rocked back and forth. My older brothers borrowed a wagon and horse to take his body to the synagogue where a burial society prepared him to be interred. The men of our community washed my father, cleaned under his nails with a small stick shaved from an orange tree and wrapped him in white linen. The rabbi was called, the burial site inside the city walls was prepared and my mother became a mourner in black for the rest of her life.

For *aveilut,* the time of mourning, we sat on low stools and pillows on the floor for a week while neighbors brought trays of home cooked food. In between, passages were read from the Zohar, a compendium of mystical teachings. My brothers tore their lapels to show they were in mourning after our father was buried. *Kriah,* that act of rendering one's clothes, was a reminder of our loss.

My mother was disconsolate, so I stepped in to perform her duties. I loved my father, too, and would miss him.

Chapter Five

With our lives in turmoil after the death of my father, my brothers fought about his routes, who would take over the business, where his lists of people were that he gave credit to, all with my mother grieving in her room. Italian lessons ended. I became the cook and maid for a household of men.

Reality shifted once more. The Aldaheff family came to pay their respects. Joseph and I exchanged greetings. His beard was scrawny as chicken's legs, his slouching shoulders slanted toward the floor and his breath unpleasant. How was I going to marry this boy?

His father, Abraham, shooed the women away so he could speak to my brothers. Joseph sat at his side. I hid behind a door while my mother waited in her room. My heart was pounding. Would they move the wedding date closer? Where would we live? Would I have to stay at his house with a family of strangers? Sweat began to pool under my arms.

Then I heard Abraham Aldaheff ask about the dowry amount. "Is it prepared and ready to deliver? We have plans to be made. Is your mother agreeable to our terms?"

Bohor cleared his throat. "Señor Alhadeff." He addressed him with an unusual formality. "My sister is ready to be married; however, with the death of my father we have had burial expenses and some other unexpected financial obligations I was not prepared for—." His voice faded as the senior Alhadeff stood and his son followed suit.

"I have had enough stalling. Your father and I made a commitment when these children were ten years of age. Now you are reneging on our agreement. Your father never would have stood for this. Do you have the full amount of the dowry or not?"

I could not see Bohor's expression, but I understood the silence. I peeked around the corner. I heard, "Consider our agreement null and void," and then a firm closing of our wooden front door, a few pink leaves spilling onto our tiles. I sunk to the floor. It wasn't that I wanted to marry Joseph, but the prospect of keeping house for my brothers for the rest of my life was not appealing either. *Why were they not married?* My friends were also promised to other young men in our community with a spate of weddings already planned. Joya was not happy about her parents' choice either, but her dowry was intact. We often murmured about what happened on the wedding night because our mothers shared so little information. But that was no longer a problem for me.

When the agreement was made six years ago, my parents knew they had time to fulfill the details of the agreement that included linens, livestock and cash. Now I was abandoned. Who would marry me? It was a scandal in our community for a promise to be broken. I would not be able to show my face in the market for months. The humiliation I felt at the Alhadeff rejection made me sink into myself.

My mother could not be a comfort. I was alone while my friends were preparing for the Purim festival, one of our happiest times.

In the past, we celebrated our freedom by indulging in food and drink, making a lot of noise and reading the *megillah*. It's the story of Queen Esther and how she convinces her evil husband, Haman, King of Persia, to save the Jews. We call our enemy, the king, Aman. My mother and I used to prepare *borekas*, a sweet morsel of dough that we stuffed with cheese or potatoes, *boulukounin* made with honey and sesame seeds and *foulares* and a hard-boiled egg we wrapped in dough to symbolize the bad king in jail. My brothers would take a tray around to the delight of neighbors.

But, what I missed the most was our tradition of the women attending the Kahal, our beautiful synagogue, on the second night with all the other women and girls in our community. The rabbi read us the entire megillah in Ladino while we sighed in recognition of the familiar story. Due to the period of mourning my mother and I did not attend

Chapter Six

In my grief for my father and myself I forgot all else, until one afternoon when there was a firm knock at the door while I was washing fresh eggplants in the sink. My mother, who was aging before our eyes, answered it. "Ah, Signore di Liscia, you have heard our sad news."

"Yes, I have come to offer my condolences."

"Please come in. May I offer you some refreshment?"

"No, I cannot stay long. My battalion is being shipped to the mainland. Mussolini wants to prepare for war."

I could not hear them once they sat in our wooden sofas plush with pillows my mother and I had embroidered. I heard the front door close. I wiped my hands on my apron and rushed out the back door to see if I could catch him. I ran to the front of our home to look for the familiar bicycle, but not it was there. I missed him. A funny feeling came over me, a rise of flutters that sped from my stomach to my chest and then my head. I felt dizzy as I pushed my hand against our stucco wall.

"Luna, are you alright?" *Where was this voice coming from?* "Luna, look at me. Are you unwell?"

My head hung to my chest while I took short breaths. My head was spinning. Then I felt a finger lift my chin and I looked into my Italian teacher's eyes. We paused for a moment. I closed my eyes as he leaned forward and kissed me, a short, sweet grazing of the lips. He took my hand and guided me to the side of the house where we would not be visible from the street.

I leaned back against the wall, my hands behind my back. A strand of hair slipped from my scarf and blew across my face. I did not say a word. He was leaning over me, his hands beside my head until he brushed the hair away from my cheek. We stared at each other. *Should this continue? Should I run away?* Frozen in place like an icy lake, I waited. He leaned to kiss me again and I turned my head. It landed on my cheek.

"Do not be afraid. I will not hurt you." With that he moved my chin toward his lips and kissed me with passion. I was shocked, yet I liked it. We separated to look at one another. He did it again. I was more compliant this time, bringing my arms to lock behind his neck.

In a moment I was back in the kitchen, heart aflutter, washing greens for a salad.

"Where were you?" My mother asked.

"The bathroom."

"Did you know the Italian naval officer came to pay his condolences?"

I shook my head no. I had not lied to my mother since I was a small child when I took extra candy from her bag. Lying was against our faith. I felt an instantaneous swoosh of guilt, a seagull lifting off with its wing span spread open to the sea.

"Your brothers are bringing home fish tonight for dinner," said my mother as she patted me on my shoulder. "Thank you for making a salad, mi ija. Did you pick tomatoes and green onions?"

"Yes, Momma. They are here," I was washing them without turning around.

Chapter Seven

My life settled into a routine. We struggled. Although we had plenty to eat, Bohor and Rodolfo fought without end over the business my father had developed with care over many years, his loyal contacts in shops, market stalls or travelers themselves. How could they make the business grow? Who should travel to Ankara in Turkey to buy more goods? There was never enough money. Women were their main customers because most sewed clothing, repaired upholstery, knitted scarves and sweaters. Notions were well-received. I assisted with sorting threads by color, buttons by size, ribbons by length and stacking seam rippers in a pile.

My mother was a dark shadow who floated through our few rooms and left only for synagogue or La Juderia near the pier on Dossiadou Street to shop and see friends. She said little to any of us. I missed her. We had been close as the only females in the household, but now I was alone. Sometimes she said to me, "I loved him very much." It gave me hope I might learn to love if I ever married. I was relieved not to be paired with the Aldaheff boy and sorry not to have a celebration. *Did we really not have enough for the dowry or did my brothers make that up to keep me at home?*

Joya stopped to see me one afternoon on her way back from the market, her basket filled with a rainbow of tomatoes in various sizes and colors. Our mothers prepared a salad with lettuce, tomato, garlic from our garden and olive oil. After all, she and her family were planning a wedding. She no longer complained about her intended. They were allowed to sit together at family gatherings, and, with modernity, allowed to talk and laugh.

"He is funny," she told me.

"What about the other?"

"My mother has given me more information."

I raised my eyebrows. "What? Tell me."

Joya blushed. "I cannot. It is embarrassing."

"Is it disgusting?" I wanted to know.

"Have you ever seen a naked man?"

I had seen my brothers after they finished their Sabbath bath in our backyard. My father constructed it and surrounded it with wooden slats. They went in together and came out with Turkish towels draped over their shoulders and wrapped around their waists. One time Rodolfo's towel slipped from his waist. Bohor pushed him out of the enclosure and from our kitchen window I saw something long and hanging surrounded by a fuzzy bush of hair. It shocked me so I continued to stare until he recovered the towel.

"No," I replied.

With confidence Joya explained the process of intercourse. I had a general idea, but now it sounded repugnant. Yes, I had seen farm animals locked together, but I did not know the details of making a baby. It was our duty to have children. Maybe never marrying was a good choice for me. "What if it hurts or you do not like it?" I probed.

Joya's expression became sanguine, a pink blush rising to her cheeks. She sighed. "I do not have expectations. My mother told me women have to endure certain things. That is what they and their mothers did before them."

"Does anyone ever like it?" the flash of my passionate kiss enveloping me.

Joya lifted her shoulders. "I do not know."

Chapter Eight

My Italian disappeared with the Royal Navy, *Regia Marina*, as we called it and *Mare Nostrum* (Our Sea) by Mussolini. He was gone for months and I tried to forget about him, but I remembered his face, the aroma when he leaned over me, his uniform, the way he sang and played guitar; a Greek god sculpted from ancient marble.

In September of 1943 the Battle of Rhodes took place between Italian and German forces. Who would have thought a battle would be named after our small island located at the tip of the Aegean Sea for over two thousand years? Italian forces took up stations around the island. It was rumored that our aircraft testing the skies were plagued by repairs. I was grateful the navy was protecting us.

However, the Germans had made their presence known since January of 1943. By April a large battalion of Germans with Panzer guns were everywhere in their armored cars. They even drafted three hundred Greek soldiers to wear their German uniform.

Later, we learned a mix up in communications from the Italian command sent leaflets over the island encouraging the Italians to take up arms against the Germans. The Germans sent their own flyers encouraging surrender for free passage to Italy. We huddled together in fear of the fighting. The Italian soldiers damaged their rifles before turning them into the enemy. They felt they had been sold out. Fortunately, Luigi was given civilian clothes to escape. More than six thousand men were declared missing because they drowned on the ships taking them away while the Germans executed ninety officers, many without a trial. I hated them.

Luigi returned with his battalion and he inquired about me among my friends. I was now an unmarried almost nineteen-year-old woman, past my prime as my brothers reminded me. When I stole a look in a small mirror my mother hid in her nightstand drawer (vanity was not admired), I saw a dark-haired young woman with large eyes and an engaging smile. I was flattered that he remembered me, but I knew it had no possibility of moving forward. I resigned myself to never having a match. No one in my family wanted it, especially my brothers who liked me to take care of the house, shop and cook. My mother assisted but she was a shadow that filled the corners of our home. I never saw her smile or laugh. She visited a few other friends who were older widows, but there was no longer any enthusiasm for life.

A few weeks later Signore di Liscia, my teacher of Italian grammar and common phrases, appeared at our door. I welcomed him in and called to my mother who was shelling beans in the kitchen. I had been reading Jewish texts about the False Messiah, Sabbatai Zvi, who fooled so many in Rhodes when he arrived in 1655. I wanted to know what he said to the rabbi to convince him. *How does one know what to believe? How could so many have been fooled?* The sad part was that the rabbi's son followed a devotee of his to the Holy Land. Much to my late father's embarrassment his ancestors followed the charlatan. It caused a rift in the family when some realized he was not the messiah because he converted to Islam. I sighed in relief that I was not part of that history.

My brothers considered it a waste of time for me to be educated, but I liked school, reading, learning. My father had encouraged me to learn more about our Sephardic history, although he claimed we had been in the Greek Islands for centuries. My father often repeated, "The Evil Queen and her feckless King Ferdinand issued their Edict in Spain in 1492 and we were dispersed around the world like seeds. We are part of the Diaspora that has sent our people to Portugal, the Ottoman Empire, Morocco, Arabic deserts, South America and many islands in the Caribbean. We are fortunate to stay in Rhodes."

"I am happy to see you again. You look well," he said.

I nodded, not quite as shy as before he left. After all, he was older too. He held my hand. The warmth of his palm traced up my arm. When my mother entered he dropped it and gave her a proper greeting. She sat down on a pillowed chair under the window.

"Where have you been?" I asked.

He gave an explanation of his maneuvers with reserve. "Some information is classified."

My mother watched. It became awkward. He addressed her, "Do you mind if I keep company with your daughter?" I had no idea what it meant; however, I assumed he wanted us to spend time together. Alone. I knew this was not allowed.

My mother spoke, "Signore, you are a gentleman and I appreciate your approach. Are you aware we are Jews? That there is no mixing of the faiths? What would your Catholic parents say?"

"My parents are gone with the influenza. My nonnina, my little Italian grandmother, and aunt raised me. I know there are unfortunate circumstances, but I want my own family. How am I to know Luna if there is not a chance for us to speak? I am very drawn to her."

"Can you not find someone of your own faith?" my mother asked with a bit of sarcasm.

"I like Luna," he stated with simplicity.

"And it is forbidden for her to marry out of our faith."

"Is there nothing I can do?"

She hesitated and then spoke with a boldness I had not seen since my father left us. "Yes, you can become a Jew."

"And that would satisfy you?"

"It would satisfy G-d."

My brothers came in through the back door and greeted my Italian with fervor. After all, we had all played music together and shared meals. Rodolfo asked, "What are you doing here?"

"I have come to ask if your sister may spend time with me, but there seems to be an obstacle."

Bohor and Rodolfo's relaxed posture shifted to stiff as they pulled themselves to their full height. "What is it?" asked Bohor.

"Your mother has informed me I must be a Jew to get to know your sister. Is that true?"

"Yes," agreed Bohor. "Our traditions honor an arranged marriage. Luna was promised but with the death of our father, plans have altered."

"But it is a modern world. We are at war. Customs change with the times. As your circumstances have." He added the last phrase with a knowing look. If my brothers could be persuaded, then options allowed possibilities.

"My family will have to discuss this. It is without precedence."

"I understand. This is what my heart wants. Do you not love your sister as well?"

My heart leaped at the word love. A flush covered my body. My mother's mouth was an "O."

My brother sat down and motioned him to a chair where they were almost knee-to-knee. Rodolfo stood behind my mother who remained seated, perhaps in shock. I could feel her panic. *My Luna, my only daughter, to marry someone who is not part of our Rhodesli community? An Italian Catholic? My husband is turning over in his grave.* She found a handkerchief in the pocket of her skirt and sniffled into it.

Bohor leaned forward, his hands on his knees. He spoke with intention, his voice rising with affront. "Are you willing to leave Catholicism to become part of our faith? How will you let go of Christ? Christmas? The Resurrection? Even the Trinity?" There was a pause in the room, as though someone lifted a hot pan from the fire.

43

"I feel more Jewish than Catholic." Luigi paused to draw a deep breath. "I want to be part of a family, a culture, one that respects life, that follows tradition. Besides, Rhodes is where I want to live after my service. There is nothing for me to go back to in my village. My grandmother has passed, my aunt, elderly. Nothing waits for me there."

The room was silent but for the tap-tap-tap of a woodpecker and voices passing in the street. I held my breath. Of course no one asked what I wanted. If my father was not able to make decisions, then my oldest brother was responsible.

"Will your family object? asked Bohor.

"I am from San Angelo del Pesco in the hills. We raised fruits and vegetables that grew well in the cooler climate. My relatives made preserves they sold in the market. Good, unsophisticated rural people. A simple life. Which is why I joined the navy. My parents died many years ago. My grandmother and aunt raised me. My auntie will be happy if I am."

"Please join us for dinner," invited Bohor, glancing at my mother and me. "This requires more discussion. Then our rabbi must be consulted before we continue."

My hands shook at the prospect of eating dinner with him, our furtive looks and brief hand holding not allowed. My mother and I rose to prepare our meal with a bit extra. My mind raced.

Could this be happening to me? To be so close? Would the rabbi allow such a thing? My brothers?

Chapter Nine

Afew weeks before the rabbi agreed to meet with Luigi, he came to see me to relate his progress. It had been agreed we could not keep company unless his conversion was complete. After he called to me through the open window, I leaned out to see him waiting, hat in hand. I wanted him to speak first so I waited.

"Luna, I spoke to your rabbi. He does not believe in my sincerity. I have to study Judaism and go before a panel of three rabbis in order to complete a conversion."

"Yes, just as I thought." I was not putting my heart into this venture because I knew he could change his mind. The tasks involved were formidable.

Luigi bowed his head. When he looked up, our eyes met, mine pooling with tears. This was what I wanted. I knew how to keep a Jewish home. Would my brothers let me leave, especially Bohor who was ten years older than me and thought he knew everything?

"Luna, will you marry me?" I could not speak. He added, "If I convert?"

Tears flowed down my face. A window and wall separated us. I wanted him to hold me. "Yes," I squeaked out. Then I realized I was not allowed to make that decision on my own. "But my brothers . . ."

"I will take care of them. My classes with the rabbi start in two days and I have work to do on the base." With that he did a small jump onto his bicycle, turned and raced down the path as my heart thumped a steady, loud beat.

Chapter Ten

I did not hear from Luigi for over a month. I wondered if he had changed his mind until I received a letter, hand delivered by one of the scrawny Greek boys who hung around the market. The envelope had his dirty fingerprints on it.

> *My dearest Luna, light of my life,*
>
> *I am sorry to have been absent from your world. Your smile keeps me sane. I have had more responsibilities on the base with Mussolini's insistence on war preparation. When I am free I race to study with the rabbi. My progress is slow. I am learning Jewish history, including the Inquisition that scattered your people all over the world. That is how your family arrived in Rhodes! Some Jews on the island are Romaniote, those who came from Rome since the beginning of time. Others came in the 1500s after the Queen Isabella unjustly threw your people out of Spain. Soon, I will be one of you. I will be a proud Jew.*
>
> *Lovingly,*
> *Your soon-to-be intended,*
> *Luigi*

I read the letter more than a few times and tucked it away in my apron pocket. His intention was clear!

The following week Luigi came to the front window strumming his guitar. A romantic serenade ensued while I was captivated with his Italian verses. My brother, Rodolfo, came up behind me to listen. When I swooned, he placed his hands around my waist. He was my sweet brother. He understood my plight, unmarried with a Gentile prospect. *What could this lead to?*

"I have come to tell you that the rabbi is questioning my motives," he said with his last strum across the strings.

"What does that mean?" I asked as a lump passed from my heart to my stomach.

"He says he cannot convert someone with ulterior motives." Rodolfo squeezed my waist.

"What does that mean? Are you not sincere in your study of Torah?"

"Yes. But he knows I want to be a Jew so that you will marry me. I have tried to explain my passion for your people and all you have endured, but it is not satisfactory."

This was bad news. If the rabbi thought he had ulterior motives, it would not happen. It was hard for me to understand. If I wanted to be Catholic, G-d forbid, then I could walk into the church and a priest would baptize me before I changed my mind! One of the girls from my class did such a thing and her parents went into mourning. I could not speak.

"Luna, maybe if Bohor expressed my sincerity to him, he would relent. He told me he had to stop my lessons unless I have a better reason than to marry the beautiful Jewess, Luna." For the first time I heard the desperation in Luigi's voice.

"Have you agreed you will accept the covenant of the Jewish people and the yoke of the Torah and complete *mitzvot*?" I asked. I had grown up in the faith, but to a new convert it had to be overwhelming. The 613 commandments called mitzvot, plus extra ones added by rabbis, were our moral and religious compass. They were more than good deeds. They were the heart of our faith for thousands of years.

Rodolfo, a witness to this conversation turned me around to face him. "Is this what you want, my dear sister?"

My eyes were flooded with tears as I nodded yes. I whispered hoarsely, "What else will I do with my life? I want to be a mother." Rodolfo pulled me toward him in an unexpected moment of affection. He held me for a minute. My thoughts raced to older girls I had known who were paired with widowers or traveling salesmen, some of whom seemed too old to father children and one who had hair growing from his ears.

"I will speak to Bohor," he told me and left.

Luigi played one last song while I wept.

That night I slept, restless with vivid dreams of a biblical woman, her head covered, a leather case in her hand. It frightened me because it seemed so real. *What could it mean?*

Chapter Eleven

Weeks slipped by until Bohor met with the rabbi. I bit my nails in desperation while waiting to hear my fate. I ran outside to greet him to garner any information. He shooed me away until we could be inside the privacy of our home. Even my mother woke up from her nap to hear whether Luigi was going to be converted or not.

Bohor sat with authority in my father's chair and leaned forward as we waited. Rodolfo, my mother and I squeezed into our ancient love seat with its threadbare rose-colored upholstery, the wood frame gleaming from decades of my mother's polishing cloth. My heart was racing. *What could it be?* Bohor cleared his throat, glanced at the floor and then back to us.

"Luigi has a consideration to his conversion that he only expressed with reservation to the rabbi. Unless he meets the *poskim* of our faith, a decision of the law only made by a scholar, there cannot be a conversion." He looked at me with his limpid brown eyes. "Nor can there be a marriage."

I began to cry, head in my hands. My only hope crushed like red grapes for wine. "Why? Has he changed his mind? What can it be?" There was an extended pause before Bohor spoke.

"Circumcision." After he said this word the room was so silent I could hear my mother's heartbeat next to me.

Finally, Rodolfo spoke. "I can understand his apprehension. It's something that happens on the eighth day after birth. We do not remember this procedure. Ah, but for an adult, it is a major decision."

"When is it supposed to take place?" I asked with a sudden flutter of practicality.

"It is after the *beit din*, the questioning panel of three rabbis. He must accept our Law of Moses, traditions, texts and agree to raise a Jewish family," said Bohor. "And, he must go into a ritual bath, the *mikvah,* and go underwater three times."

After wiping my tears with a handkerchief from my pocket, I sat with my hands folded in my lap. I understood his hesitation. It was one thing for a baby to have a *brit*, but another for an adult. The few I had attended were emotional, joyful celebrations to celebrate the oldest covenant between man and G-d. After all, Abraham was the first. Wait. He was in his nineties according to biblical texts. *Why could not this man who professed his love for me, in his twenties, not do this?* The silence in the room continued until my mother wriggled her way out of the decrepit cushions of the loveseat to go into the kitchen. Since the death of my father she rarely smiled. It was difficult to know what she was thinking, although I believed she wanted me to be happy. I was, after all, her only daughter, after she had birthed five children.

he slid to the crown of his head and waited for me in the front of our synagogue. My mother and her friends had crafted a gown of white silk and pearl buttons from my late father's inventory and added a diaphanous veil. Bohor walked me down the aisle until I stood under the canopy, my father's prayer shawl, symbolizing a Jewish home, wrapped around us. My mother stood on one side and Joya, my dearest friend, stood on the other while the rabbi intoned the marriage vows. Lifting my eyes to my groom, as part of tradition, I circled him seven times to respect the seven days of creation and the loneliness of his soul. I breathed a sigh of relief when the glass cracked under his heel, a symbol of the destruction of the temple. My kiss was tender like none other. I was married!

Chapter Twelve

With the pressure of war building Luigi and I stayed at my home. He still had to sleep at the base except for our wedding night. I was self-conscious as my mother helped me undress and put on a fresh nightgown. Luigi and my brothers sat drinking on our back porch after a small reception at the temple. I could hear shuffling of feet and their laughter. After a while, they broke into song.

My mother put her arms around me, "Luna, my lovely Luna, you have been a helpmate to me. Now it is time to start a family."

"But mama, I do not know what to do tonight, what to expect. I'm afraid."

She hugged me again. "There is nothing to fear. You will be uncomfortable but it is your duty. That is how you will have children, beautiful babies who will love you, ones that are G-d given gifts."

My new husband and brothers got louder and I heard a toast, "To the Jews of Rhodes," and then more shouts.

By the time Luigi made his way inside to share my parents' bed with me—Mama had insisted she move into my smaller room—I was asleep. I felt his warm breath on my neck as his hands reached for my breasts. The un-sweet smell of wine on his breath made me fake rest. What happened next did not surprise me. He fell asleep. When I awoke in the morning I was still a virgin. I was relieved. At least my brothers could not tease me about strange noises that Joya told me was a giveaway.

That day and many others were the same. Luigi left early before the light slithered through the shutters to be at his naval base; my brothers checked the docks for shipments and sent out reminders to those who owed them money or goods. Mama shopped, gardened and prepared dinners with my help. It was like being single except when Luigi surprised us, out of breath from the long bike ride. We greeted each other with kisses on both cheeks and a moment to stare into each other's eyes.

We washed our hands, said blessings over the bread and wine and sat down for a meal, usually filled with joy and prayer. We consummated the marriage; however, it wasn't as terrible as I thought, nor was it pleasurable as the first kisses. He was a gentle lover, always seeking pleasure for both of us. I loved him.

Four months after the wedding, I got sick. I awoke late and felt so nauseous I could not sit up to make it to the wash stand. I vomited on the floor. I called out with weakness to my mother who rushed to the doorway of her old bedroom. I kept her room because we never knew when Luigi would show up. She looked at me and the floor and she knew what I did not. I was with child.

She returned with a wet rag to wipe my mouth and a pan to clean the mess I made. She sat on the edge of the bed and held me in her arms. I cried. I knew. She pulled back to look at me and smiled. "You will be a wonderful mother." She paused as my eyes filled with tears. "And I am thrilled to be a nonna!" We put our arms around each other and wept, me because I was so inexperienced and she, because she missed my father.

Chapter Thirteen

1938

While my brothers celebrated the Italian national football team's World Cup for the second time, Luigi and I had some romantic moments strolling to the water with our new daughter, Carmelina, standing at the pier, watching the ships dock. The world was in turmoil with Mussolini's demands and Hitler's threats, but it did not touch me. I was a married woman with a good-looking Italian *Jewish* husband and a baby. I have to say he adapted to our rituals and traditions with ease. He was observant on Shabbat, wearing his kippah in the house and taking charge of the wine. Bohor and Rudolfo liked having him around. We played music after dinner now that I was allowed to sing and play my mandolin with him. My mother fussed over the baby, making a tiny wreath of cloth flowers as a crown for her, sewing precious clothes and buying miniature leather shoes for her in the market. Carmelina, named after my mother's mother, was adored.

But it did not last long. Luigi was called back to his base for weeks at a time and we were not allowed to know what was happening. The

Spanish Civil War started in July of 1936, a shock to all of us. Within days Spain was split in two. The following month word reached us that Federico Garcìa Lorca, the well-known poet, was executed. Joya and I grieved because we had studied his poems at home. Luigi told me the fascists committed the crime and banned his work. Thank Goodness we were safe on Rhodes where his forbidden book was under my mattress. His gentle words comforted me when I sat up late nursing Carmelina. I did not know enough to take sides. But I knew this writer was an asset to his fellow citizens.

Later, when all was said and done, I learned more than a half a million people were killed in the Spanish Civil War and that Jews played a large part. Many of the foreign recruits from Poland, America and Britain as well as most of the medical personnel joined the International Brigades. I prayed we would never see such violence on our island paradise.

When the Italians first arrived in 1912, our community greeted them as liberators from the Turks. I was young so I liked the celebrations. But, it was short-lived. The appointed civilian governor, Mario Lago, had a vision to impose Italian culture on us, which most of our community did not mind. He restored medieval buildings, encouraged tourists and banned the Greek language with its Orthodox church. Many Italian families settled on our island and we welcomed them. After all, I had a special status. I was married to one! Mario Lago united the Turkish, Greek and Jewish parts of our island, increasing prosperity for all. We looked upon him with kindness. He did not interfere with our Jewish lives so we saw him as benevolent until he was removed by a Fascist in 1936. The Italians had aligned with Germany in June of that year. By December Mario de Vecchi di

Val Cismon was appointed governor of the Dodecanese Islands, a group of twelve islands and many smaller ones off the coast of Turkey known for their sunshine.

Rhodes was the greenest because natural springs dotted the landscape creating ribbons of water down the hills that fed crops, fruit trees and wild flowers.

In rapid succession the Rabbinical College closed. Jews could no longer close their shops on the Sabbath or for holidays. One hundred tombstones were removed from the cemetery to enhance de Vecchi's new home, and, the worst insult, the leaders of our community were required to visit him on Rosh Hashanah, the Jewish New Year. In the past the governor came to the synagogue to wish them well on the holy day.

Everything was under construction. The Italians demolished the small homes built near the city walls and tore down other Ottoman buildings. They even established an Institute for the Study of History and Culture, modernized our roads and built an aquarium in the popular art deco style that had been admired since the first war. But, by far, their grandest structure was the Palace of the Grand Master of the Knights of Rhodes in our medieval old town. We had called it the *Kastello* forever. It had functioned as a palace, headquarters and a fortress by the Knights Hospitaller in the 1300s. My brothers believed that it was the same site where the original giant statue, the Colossus of Rhodes, stood from the Hellenistic period, but their friends argued with them about its origins. After all, we were an ideal port for the meeting of the Mediterranean and Aegean seas. By the time the Italians arrived it was damaged. I watched the repairs with interest, Carmelina's tiny hand in mine.

It seemed the world was re-arming itself while the Italian Navy launched two new battleships in 1937, the "Littorio" and the "Vittorio Veneto." Luigi was assigned to the first. I knew I might not see him for a long time after he received his orders, especially since he was called to participate in the trials. It had to be sea-worthy.

Meanwhile, Luigi's bunkmates gave him a hard time about converting to Judaism. There were still vestiges of farm boy fears about Jews, but he was smart and patient. He took the time to explain the prayers he said on Friday night if he was not in our home. After a while they left him alone. A few who saw me in the market told him he had made a good choice. They were mostly boys from small villages who joked about snipping their penises to find someone like me. It was a strange arrangement but war was in the air and no one wanted to die.

It was only a matter of time before Luigi received his orders. He barely made it back to the base on our last night together. We had learned to keep our lovemaking silent with so many of us in the house, but I felt something. I knew something. No tearful good-bye. Just the gathering of clothes in his arms, a kiss for the baby, the squeaky wheel of his bicycle and he was gone. And, I was with child again.

Chapter Fourteen

September 1938

The anti-Jewish laws put in place by the Italian government shocked us. Many of our neighbors and synagogue members fled our paradise. It was reported more than 2000 left. That was half our population! Many young single men left their families for Africa with promises to return and send news. They settled in Rhodesia's capital, Salisbury. Most of us were poor without much hope so leaving was difficult. We were sad to see our community fractured.

When I hugged Joya and Maria, my childhood friends, good-bye, we all cried. We had played near the sea, gathered peaches and berries in the hills, worshipped together with other women in the balcony, married and given birth within a short span of time of each other. Our lives had been a fairytale until now, one with beautiful princesses and handsome princes, glorious holidays with abundant food, candles shimmering shadows onto our stone walls. They were part of the warm bosom that was my Rhodes family. Joya and Maria were my sisters. When they left on a boat with their families along with 300 others for Haifa, I was bereft. Tears seeped from my eyes for days while I changed linens, washed baby clothes and helped my mama with the cooking. I avoided the market because I knew I would not find my friends there. I was a married woman, no longer being brought up on an idyllic island. Who would protect us now?

The Count Cesare Maria de Vecchi instituted new rules with haste. We knew he was a fascist without respect for our history. He abolished not just our courts but also the Muslim and Greek Orthodox ones too. In fact, his high-handed attitude made many hate him, especially the Greeks who were forced to speak Italian along with other indignities. One of which, I experienced myself.

I was out walking with the babies in the cooler morning air, plodding with effort because my belly was so big. Number three. That's what happens when your husband comes home on leave and you make good use of your time. Besides, we hid in the house so no one would see us. Luigi did not like the new rules either. We spent hours whispering in bed while nonna kept the children busy. He told me not to worry, that the Italians would win the war and all would be the same on our island again.

When I heard a horn blast, I jumped, fearful I had stepped into the path of a vehicle. Carmelina started crying. I held her hand tight. I picked up Isaac from his buggy as I looked around. An enormous black limousine pulled up across from where we stood. I wiped Carmelina's wet face with the end of my shawl and hoisted my baby boy, higher on my hip. With a screeching of brakes the other cars and wagons stopped, people left their vehicles, standing at attention and there was fear on their faces. *What did this mean?* A back door was opened, and knee-high black boots stretched out into the street. A short man in a black shirt, khaki pants and a cummerbund got out to stand at attention. His walrus-sized mustache made him look the fool. People who had emptied out of their cars did the same, their backs straight in fear. And then I saw something I never thought would happen.

He offered a Fascist salute and those of us on the street were expected to return the "Heil Hitler." I could not do it. My hands were not free because of the babies. I tussled their little bodies and a few packages in my arms. I looked around and saw a store I could duck into within a few steps. I prayed no one saw me disobeying De Vecchi, especially him. So many had suffered indignities at his hands. It was rumored that the Duce himself, was angry at his cruelty and ineptitude.

I entered the store with two wailing children and looked around. It was a Greek shoemaker's shop with the proprietor sitting behind the counter cobbling a heel on a boot. The aroma of black boot caught my nostrils.

"What's all the noise about?" he asked, thrusting his chin toward the door.

I had to be careful not to express my disgust. One never knew outside our Sephardic community who was a friend or foe. "Di Vecchi stopped his limousine so we may honor him."

The shoemaker took his eyes away from his task to look at me with wide, dark eyes. He spit on the floor next to him. We did not need to talk to express how we felt about the newest leader of the Italian occupation. Frozen, I observed the few people who were returning his salute in the street. I did not want to leave while he was still there in his ridiculous Storm Trooper boots. Finally, I gathered my babies and packages to move toward the door.

"Have you seen the villa Di Vecchi is building for Il Duce?" the shoemaker asked me. I didn't know if it was a trap. We were all suspicious. I nodded.

"It's a two-story mansion with views of the Aegean Sea. He started a few years ago. The Villa de Vecchi is supposed to be another palace." He shared this news with an undertone of annoyance.

"Yes, I know of this." And to myself, *we are watching from below as our resources are wasted.*

With more insult the governor removed all our Ladino street names. Our Calle Ancha also known as La Kaye Ancha became Piazza Principe Umberto di Savoia and Calle de Talmud Torah became Via Melichore Asinari. A travesty. In private conversations we never called them by their new names. We called them by our beloved ones.

And, as if the indignities were not enough, in the midst of this devastation our new authoritarian ordered that our graveyard inside the city walls, the one where my father was interred, had to be moved south a few kilometers away on the road to Kalitheas. Rumors spread that he wanted the gravestones to build gardens for his new palace, Il Castello. We were appalled. My mother sobbed for days. Endless discussions ensued about whether the body should be disinterred or whether we should just move the gravestone. My brothers argued so much I forgot who was supporting which side, all while my mother's musical crying, an opera of grief, filled up our rooms. One thousand gravestones had to be transferred to the new site. The senior Alhadeff cousins who owned the bank supervised the move for most, a difficult task with mourners insisting they walk behind the trucks and carts. It was as though those who were interred had died again. We could only move the headstone. Finally, Bohor and Rudolfo rented a donkey and wagon from a Greek peasant to move my father's tombstone to the new cemetery. None of this made my mother feel any better. She wailed the refrain, "Hashem, help us. What has happened to our community?"

After the humiliation of moving my father's headstone, something else happened that truly shocked us. The governor had new decrees. Within a short time he closed the rabbinical college, forced shops to stay open on Saturdays and banned the slaughtering of animals in the kosher way, which was more humane. The one that affected our family the most: all Jews who had Italian citizenship had to leave in six months.

What did this mean for Luigi? Was he supposed to leave even though he was part of the Italian navy? What about me and our two children? I was a twenty-six-year old mother with no place to go. The people who left were fortunate. We remained.

Chapter Fifteen

May 1939

I had strange visitations in my dreams. A woman and child pleaded with me, large haunted eyes, intense. She wore a necklace of gold and carried a leather bag. She has appeared in my dreams before. Or maybe they were visions. *What did they want? Were my fears invading my thoughts at night?* I awoke next to the baby gurgling in his crib and the shouting of male voices outside.

"Quick. Come. We need help. Jews have to be rescued." I did not move until I heard "Jews" and sat up. My mother stood in the doorway grabbing information as people fled to the docks. I dressed in a hurry, kissed Carmelina and Isaac, fed the baby and handed her to my mother.

A boat had stopped on our shores with 600 Jews from Prague and Braslava (I had never heard of Jews in Slovakia!) on its way to Palestine. A fire had broken out so the passengers disembarked to sleep in our stadium. I had never seen such poor Jews, many with yellow stars sewn to their chests. Even small children. The men were

71

wearing pants with rope to hold them up, shirts with the collars torn off and shoes repaired with cardboard and twine. The women, had on layers of sweaters over blouses and long skirts, many still wearing aprons, as though they left in the middle of a meal. Many were thin as a church spire. I did not know eastern European Jews were so destitute because no matter our circumstances in Rhodes, we always had enough to eat. The children were so sad, dejected and somewhat dirty. No one had taken the time to clean sleep from eyes, tangles from hair and stains splashed onto clothes.

I thought of my beautiful Carmelina, the way her nonna dressed her for Shabbat, her curls that we brushed every day, her chortles of delight. They came down the gangplank to load onto waiting trucks, their possessions in rucksacks or shabby valises. I could not stop staring at one family who could have been us, a tall, handsome clean-shaven father and his wife, a paler version of me and their little one. She, too, held a baby in her arms.

We were held behind a rope but I could not stop myself from reaching out to them as they breezed by me obeying the Italian soldiers' shouts to keep moving. The wife looked at me and our eyes met. I tried to speak a few words, but she shook her head. She did not understand my Ladino and I could not speak Czech or Yiddish. Truthfully, we knew the terrible situation the Jews were in from Germany and surrounding areas. I had been a good geography student, but I could not comprehend the danger they must have been in to escape with so little and to flee so far away, especially on the Pentcho, a ship that was in terrible condition. What must it have been like for them to see us in our starched white lace, long skirts and flowers woven in our hair?

I felt an affinity for this little family like my own, but I could not communicate with the mother. If I could I would have asked about recipes, her children, where she and her husband met. I watched for a while longer and then ran home. I had to know who they were. My mother tried to stop me as I grabbed an old square scarf and packed it with challah left from Shabbat, cheese, some greens from our garden, a small jar of preserved peaches and a bottle of wine I wrapped in old newspaper.

"Luna, what are you doing? Where are you going with these things?"

"Mama, there are poor Jews that arrived on a ship at the pier. They're from Europe wearing yellow stars. They're on their way to Palestine."

"Luna, you cannot feed an entire ship. Hundreds were on board."

"Yes, I know, but I can help one family." I went over to look in her face and hold her arms.

"Mama, this family looks like us—a tall father, a sweet mother with a baby in her arms and a precious little girl. How can I not bring them something after a long journey? Their supplies were so meager."

"Luna, my dear Luna, you cannot fix the world with a little food. Stop. Put it all back. You will not be able to find them among hundreds in the stadium."

"Mama, I have to go. You do not understand the desperation I saw on their faces. We can spare a little."

"Mi ija, the Italian soldiers will not let you in to look for them. Ach, it is my fault you are so naïve. My friends in the market heard that the steam boiler blew up between Crete and Rhodes. It hit a volcanic island and sunk."

"Mama, you cannot scare me. I'm going. I'm an adult." I did not want to push her but she stood in my way.

"I forbid you." She crossed her arms across her well-endowed bosom still draped in black silk and dared me.

I had to make a decision. She was a formidable opponent and I rarely went up against her. Only my brothers could insist with her. I relaxed my body and leaned against the kitchen table. I decided to capitulate. For the time-being. I could sneak out in the early hours of dawn and deliver my package.

All night I tossed and turned, fully dressed. I put my shoes on in darkness and felt my way into the kitchen where I had stored my goods. Somehow I slipped out without waking the baby. Another would be here in a few months. *What if those people were us?*

Chapter Sixteen

I walked through our back gate to avoid arousing our neighbor's dog and started walking with haste toward the stadium. It was far and built near the outskirts of town. I stayed close to the shadow bathed walls. I had abandoned my bottle of Rhodesian wine. Too heavy. I learned that the refugees had all gotten off the sunken ship, only to be trapped on another island for ten days without supplies.

When I got there, Italian sentries were positioned outside. I could hear the commotion inside—weeping women, crying babies, people speaking so many languages I did not understand. Above it all, I heard fervent voices murmuring the Shema, cracked with tears, the prayer elevated in the chaos. What must these people think is happening? I waited to collect my thoughts. I had to be a bold, brave, carrier of faith.

I approached the soldier with the red sash. "Signore, might I be able to deliver these goods to my cousins?" He looked me up and down and I self-consciously tucked a stray hair into my scarf.

"And who are you?"

"I am Signora Eleonora di Liscia."

"And your cousins' names?"

I was stumped. I had no idea. I decided to describe them instead. "They're a small family. The children looked so hungry when they got off the boat."

He smirked at me. "Everyone is hungry after a long journey. What do you have for them?" His chin rose in curiosity.

I unknotted my handkerchief and he poked through the few things. He picked up the challah. "What is this?"

Before I could answer the sentry on the other side of the door poked his head over to look at the goods. "It's Jew bread."

I stepped back at his effrontery. I had never heard it called that. The second soldier who was older and beefier around the middle, came close to my face. "These people do not need food. Did you not see how fat some of them are?"

I stared at my dusty shoes. It had been a mistake to come. My mother, older and smarter, knew more about hostilities. My life had been so insulated. I wished Luigi was here to assist me.

"Look," I lifted my head to meet his eyes. I'm married to an Italian in the navy." I almost blurted out he was away on maneuvers but thought better of it.

"So? Does that give you the right to come in and disrupt our refugees?"

76

Before I could think of a clever retort another soldier appeared, probably a commanding officer from the ribbons on his jacket. The two sentries explained what was going on and I was thrilled I had studied enough Italian to understand. Except they did not prove to be gentlemen. The officer came over, looked at my meager gifts, put the jar of peach preserves in his hand, juggling it back and forth and walked away. My heart stopped pounding long enough to skip a beat.

The officer turned, "Let her come in for ten minutes. If she does not find her cousins, then kick her out. Or keep her and send her on the ship with them!" The sentries laughed.

The older one threatened me. "You can come in, but we are not going to let you leave unless you come back to this door in the allotted time. Otherwise, you will be shipped to the God-forsaken desert with the Arabs!" The laughing of the two men rang in my ears.

I entered through a sheet that covered the doorway by pushing it to one side. I almost choked. The smell of hundreds of people in a small space without toilet facilities or water was overwhelming. It was a scene out of Dante's hell, a forbidden book I read, something I could never have imagined. Yellow stars blurred my vision. I had never seen so many desperate, hungry people. *How would I ever find the little family in ten minutes?*

I had no idea how long ten minutes was without a clock, but I started to trail my eyes over the top rows first. Nothing except misery. I did the next row down looking for the tall man and his pretty wife. Nothing. A *minyan* of men in black coats gathered in a corner, their bodies swaying to the rhythm of prayers, a private dance with G-d. I was fascinated with their concentration in the bedlam of humanity.

Then an old woman came up to me begging for food. I could tell she was speaking something like Hebrew and then realized it was Yiddish. I knew it was the language of European Jews, but I could not understand or speak it. We Sephardis kept ourselves separate from Ashkenazis, our eastern European cousins who lived in colder climes. We had our customs, spices, celebratory foods, Ladino language and the history of the Iberian coast. My father reminded me growing up when he returned with stories of his travels that other Jews were the same as us. "We all believe in the same G-d, my Luna, so we are all the same. Never forget who you are."

Another old woman dressed in black approached me, not unlike the widows on our island. "I am sorry. I cannot help. I am looking for my cousins." Suddenly, she grabbed my skirt in her arthritic fingers. I did not understand the words but I knew she was begging. I felt terrible. If I opened the food to give her a spray of greens I would have hundreds upon me.

It did not take long before I was surrounded with a few others. It was moments before a man grabbed my handkerchief and ran into the stands. Gone. Just like the birds that pecked at dead fish on the shore. I was a carcass.

Sensible and frightened as my time limit passed, I did not want to leave my Rhodes family to disappear on a ship. I gathered the corners of my skirt and ran toward the entrance with people trailing behind me, shouting G-d knows what. I made it through the sheet to the other side breathless. How was I to know the dangers involved with hungry, desperate people?

"Aha, so our little Jew-lover has returned," the first sentry said, sarcasm in his voice. "Leaving us so soon?" I did not want to engage. I leaped past them and ran, knowing they could not leave their post. I heard the older one yell at my back in Italian, "Are you sure you would not like to stay?"

I cried all the way home for those poor people, for my stupidity at attempting something so foolish, for my babies who might never know peace, for the sad state of the world, for my Luigi far away on a boat and for a life I saw starting to fray at the edges. We, too, were feeling the effects of war.

Chapter Seventeen

What I did not know was that others had also talked their way inside who spoke the languages of the people trapped inside. Many spoke Ladino and some Yiddish. At the market, no longer a joyous social errand, one of the older Aldaheff sisters of my long-ago-intended, stopped to whisper next to me as we picked through onions at a stall. Rebecca, a heavy-set woman with a lined face, was known for her many brilliant children, all who excelled at Torah. I did not praise them in case she believed in the evil eye. Superstitions abound in our community, especially in the older generations. My nonna, a believer in *konsejas*, folk tales, home remedies and amulets, warned me about evil spirits, telling me she sat up all night with my brothers before their brit. She even made me an amulet with a sprig of rue I wore under my blouse for a time. Sometimes I believed she was the one sending me a woman in my dreams to warn me. But of what?

I knew my intended, Joseph, had become a rabbi, married a girl with an appropriate dowry and left for America. Seattle, I think. I had no regrets. Luigi was my true love. I touched my hand underneath my belly as a reminder it all turned out well.

Rebecca saw my gesture, "What number is this?"

"Three," I answered with pride, although I knew that was not what we were taught. Humility was preferred. Besides, was it not a miracle every time?

"And, what are the others?"

I recited the ages of my baby boy and girl. "Does Joseph have children?"

"Yes, he is the father of five so far." She was proud of her brother's success. She was almost my sister-in-law. No matter. I got what I wanted. She stared at me for a moment. Was there regret in her tone? "Do you know what the Jews from the ship Pentcho are saying at the athletic stadium?"

"No, what? I tried to bring food."

She turned to face me directly. "Have you not heard the stories they're telling about what is happening to European Jewry?"

"No." I felt a panic of indigestion rustle inside of me. Sweat dripped down my hairline onto my forehead. I felt warm all over. I did not want to faint. The smells and shouts in the market started to make me dizzy. I did not want to show weakness here, especially in front of Rebecca.

"The Germans are murdering Jews in forests where they dig their own pits first. There are trucks brought to gas people. Women, babies. Everyone."

I put my hands over my ears. "Stop."

Rebecca ceased speaking. I could not absorb what she was telling me. I dropped my onions and stumbled away, tears streaming down my face. Cruelty was not something I knew or understood. On a small island in a shielded community we followed the rabbinical teachings of loving kindness. *Does my mother know this? Luigi? Why is this happening?*

Later I learned everything she told me was true, confirmed by neighbors. It was our first inkling of what was happening to our people. We were grieving for those trapped in our stadium, their lost luggage in the shipwrecked boat near the island of Samos and the conditions where they stayed, forced to live like frenzied animals caught in a trap. Our community organized a way to bring food, blankets and other useful supplies like buckets and toilet paper. I smuggled in my prayer book when I eventually found the woman I saw leaving the ship and her elegant husband. She cried when I handed it to her, placing it close to her heart. She asked me a question I did not understand.

I turned to another woman who was with me. She translated the Czech for me. "Why are we being treated this way? We have done nothing wrong."

I could not reply. Tears filled my eyes. I knew so little of the world and its ways. Nothing prepared me for this. I hugged her, left through the only entrance in the front and collapsed against the outside of the building to cry, head in hands. *Why was this happening? Who was responsible?*

After a few months the three hundred refugees were gone. Just like that. A new transport ship arrived and they sailed to Palestine. At the time none of us knew how lucky they were.

Chapter Eighteen

May, 1940

One year later our idyllic island had changed drastically. First, I had another little boy we named Joseph, after my father. He was a happy baby although not as lively as the other two. Maybe it was his diet. We could still buy fish from the Greeks who took their boats and nets out in any kind of weather, but the best catches were taken for the occupiers. My mother and I tended our vegetable garden that gave us zucchini, lettuce, eggplants and tomatoes if we could keep the bugs off. We traded thyme and oregano with our neighbors for cumin and curry. We were never hungry but our diets had deteriorated into monotony. I missed the spices my father used to bring home from his travels.

I saw Luigi when he visited on leave but it was infrequent. He'd only seen the new baby once. He managed to extrapolate a few extra days to stay for his son's brit. But, our time alone was intense, as though angels swept down so we could enjoy pleasures of the flesh before we slept. And then he was gone again, my sometimes lover and husband.

Rudolfo had a radio in the room he shared with Bohor where he could tune into the BBC. None of us were fluent in English, but we would invite other neighbors, the Guzmans, over to translate for us. They had relatives in America and harbored dreams of visiting them one day, although the Guzmans were elderly. We would gather in his room as he pulled the radio out of a closet from underneath floor boards. The neighbors sat on his bed, the children and I on the floor, as Rodolfo twisted and turned the knobs through screeches and crackles, with a cigarette hanging from his lips. The couple argued back and forth about the translations of words, what the information meant and after long deliberations, shared what they decided we should know. Through tight lips Mister Guzman told us the Germans had crossed the French border a few days before and were on their way to take Paris.

We were silent. Then we all spoke at once. The Germans, the Nazis, those despicable monsters, were taking over the world. Poland had fallen last September within a month. Soldiers on horses could not fight tanks. My mother wept. "Thank G-d your father did not have to endure this." I put my arms around her and held her.

My brother, Bohor, took over to quiet us down. "These are very troubled times, but I think we're safe. Who's going to bother us on a small island community? Rhodes is a place of beauty and peace. We must remember—"

I interrupted. "But what about the terrible stories we've heard about shooting Jews in forests and stories of work camps? Is someone going to protect us? Are we going to be slaves again like in Egypt?" And then I uttered an abomination. "Where is G-d?" My mother rushed from the stuffy room, the Guzmans left, too, and my brothers offered no consolation. They did not know either.

Chapter Nineteen

December 8, 1941

From my brother's secret radio and neighbors we learned that the United States had declared war on Japan. The war arena was growing into a worldwide theater, the phrase they used on a broadcast. Would the world forget about our precious island abundant with flowers, fruits, pastoral animals, the sea and good, kind people? In July of the same year Germany and its ally, Italy, declared the end of Yugoslavia. Who were they to decide an entire country, populations in cities and rural areas, were not allowed to be who they were? I ricocheted between obliviousness to the terrifying news I felt creeping closer, a reverberating panic of beats that repeated in my mind "what if." *What if Luigi did not make it through the war? What if the Nazi offensive came to our island? What if we could not escape? What if we were forced to leave like other refugees with bundles and a small valise?* Sometimes I trembled at the answers my questions might bring.

I tried not to allow myself to fall into an abyss of despair by telling myself that Luigi would return safe and rescue all of us; that we would live in a home away from my family so that we would make sweet love in our own bed. I pushed the scary thoughts away and focused on prayer, meal preparation with my mother and the impossibility of Germans being interested in less than two thousand Jews on an island. "Absurd," my rabbi told me when I expressed my doubts and fears. We went on as before. I received a letter from Luigi.

> *Dearest Luna, my love,*
>
> *I cannot tell you where I am but I am not so far away. I think of you every day. My duties are repetitive and boring, yet I am a good navy man. When will this war end? (The next part was covered in black so I couldn't read it.) Il Duce is a strong leader although many see him as a dictator. I am loyal to the Italians. I want to defend my country, but I still want to come home to your arms, under the covers, my lips pressed to yours. (The next part was censored too.) I pray we do not declare war on the U.S. May my absence from you and my children be short.*
>
> *Love,*
>
> *Luigi*

The letters from my dear husband sustained me; however, I felt so unsure about our future. *What would happen when Luigi finally came home? Would he expect me to move to Italy?* I could never leave my family even if I complained daily about our close quarters. One bathroom for four adults and three children was cramped. I dreamt about a villa wrapped in rose-colored bougainvillea with glinting sprays from a courtyard fountain, large bedrooms with tiled floors and Turkish rugs, a garden for Shabbat dinners and a kitchen with appliances where we could prepare food for feasts.

I missed my friends too.

Joya sent me a letter that stated Haifa was a place of confusion. "The city is filled with refugees from Europe, destitute and hungry, who gather on corners begging for anything; grifters who work the crowds to make a few bucks; religious zealots who approach me braying about the "end of times;" and so many languages I cannot understand." We missed each other. As girls we thought we'd live near each other forever, our family histories intertwined.

Chapter Twenty

Luigi wrote me censored letters, I repeatedly read how much he loved me, that my lips tasted like sweet wine and how much he missed my cooking. The good parts of what he wanted to do to my body were censored, even though I held them to the light. It wasn't enough. Sometimes I cried myself to sleep because I missed his warmth, his musical voice, the way he made me laugh and the depth of his commitment. Every time I thought about what he did to become Jewish so we could wed, I shivered. What a man! And now he was off fighting in a war that I knew was probably futile. Mussolini, the monster.

My brothers wanted to join the resistance, but my mother nixed that idea because they were supporting us with notions of buttons, lace, ribbons, zippers and some textiles, especially gossamer silks that I assisted in folding on a sheet on our living space floor. They could still travel to small towns and villages like Lindos on our island and sent out shipments often to the mainland. In fact, one of our

Marcia Fine

customers was the Vatican! The Pope and cardinals dressed well and needed velvet to wear inside their chilled walls. We were grateful. It also meant our packages were sent.

Much of the time, however, my brothers stayed out back in our yard smoking and drinking. They did not want to attract the notice of the military. They considered joining the Greek Army, but without kosher food and a reputation for not being treated fairly, they kept out of sight of the authorities unless necessary. Until, I learned that they both had girlfriends among the older nurses in hiding. I caught them sneaking out late one night when I was up with a crying baby.

"Where are you going?" I confronted them.

"None of your business," replied Bohor, carrying a rucksack of food he had gathered from baskets of produce near the sink.

"Why are you defiant with me? I'm not going to turn you in."

Rudolfo chimed in, a hand against Bohor's chest in an effort to push him back. "Lower your voices. We do not need to wake *vava*."

"Tell her nothing," hissed Bohor, a mean expression danced around his mouth.

"No, we have to share what we're doing, argued Rudolfo."

I looked from one to the other. What were they referring to? We lived under the same roof. I knew what was going on. Or did I? I had wondered why two handsome Jewish men were not courting some of our remaining island's beauties. But, I had assured myself they felt an obligation to support their mother and sister. Ha!

"I want to know where you are going in the dead of night. It's dangerous. What if someone catches you and thinks mama and I are involved too?" I got weepy while patting the baby's back.

"Rudolfo, let's go. We can tell her later." He pulled his arm, the rucksack swung over his shoulder.

"No!" I stomped my foot. The baby had stopped crying, thank Goodness.

Rudolfo told Bohor, "We have to tell her so we can leave. We're wasting time." Then he turned to me. "We are bringing food to the partisans in the mountains. We have to travel by foot instead of donkey so we do not attract attention."

I was shocked.

I had no idea that, other than the illegal radio, that they were supporting the partisans. "Does nonna know?"

"Of course not," Bohor said with spite. "That's it. Let's go."

"No, I want Luna to know in case something happens to us," explained Rudolfo.

My oldest brother sighed and turned his back to us, muttering curse words in Ladino and Greek.

Rudolfo took my hand. "My dearest Luna, you and your children bring joy into our lives during this terrible time. Some day Bohor and I want to have families." He paused and licked his lips. "We have girlfriends in the Resistance."

"Who?" I demanded to know. I felt outrage at their secrets.

Bohor informed me, "We cannot tell you names for your own protection."

"But you are endangering our whole family, vava, my children. How could you put us in harm's way?"

Rudolfo spoke with molasses on his tongue. "Because we have to. If we do not leave now with our food, no one will be safe." He moved toward the door and Bohor moved ahead of him. In a moment they were gone and I could only hear harsh whispers fading into the night. Later I learned our Turkish milkman, a good soul, guided them to the caves where partisans hid. When we were bombed by the Germans, and sometimes the Allies who wanted to destroy our port near the Juderia, some Jews ran to the caves to sleep on the blanketed floors.

News was scarce because we were afraid to use the radio, but a neighbor smuggled us a newspaper. On June 3, 1942, the Battle of Midway occurred that was called "the turning point of the war" in the Pacific. Apparently, the United States had intelligence that it was going to happen and they were prepared, especially since Pearl Harbor had been a surprise. All I knew was after a year at war, 35,000 soldiers in uniform were dead.

Chapter Twenty-One

August, 1943

With the Jewish New Year approaching the breezes swept our sand into small dunes and we continued without fear. After all, I was married to an Italian. My mother, the children's nonna in Italian and vava in Ladino, had shriveled into a coffee bean of black. I remained positive that all would remain calm. No warnings about the suspicion of quiet before a storm, which we knew all too well. Sometimes the palm fronds would rustle a bit and stillness settled over us.

As a child I played outside until the first fat raindrops struck me like bird poop. I would stick out my tongue to catch them and run as fast as I could to the warmth of my home. Each time I arrived with my clothes plastered to my skin, my mother peeled them from me while I shivered. We did not have a tub, only a small outside shower, which I couldn't use in the rain. My brothers would roll a banded wooden tub into the kitchen that my mother filled with boiling water half-way. Then she topped it off with rain water from the cistern positioned on our outside patio. The warm water eased over me up to my neck. I shut out my mother's harangue about getting sick by slipping under the water. Later in life I did the same in the mikvah.

At the beginning of 1943, we thought it would be over soon. Little did we know that the war had escalated. Hunched over with our ears near the speakers, we listened to my brothers' hidden radio. The Allies bombed Rome on July 19, 1943. The United States President Roosevelt and the British Prime Minister counseled the Italians not to support Mussolini and save their Italian civilization, but it was no use. The news reported panic. People poured into Rome thinking no one would dare to bomb the holy seat. They were wrong! The railroads were attacked by the Americans, especially Stazione Terminal, the main railway station, made of manufactured steel in anticipation of a World's Fair that never materialized. A working class part of the city, San Lorenzo, was destroyed. Thousands of Italian citizens were killed, people just like me and my family. I left the room before I heard anymore.

I had mixed feelings. Of course I wanted the Allies to win so we would no longer be occupied, yet, I felt Italian and although I hadn't been to Rome, I knew it was an ancient, historical city. It was the first place the Jews congregated. Some on our island were descended from them. They were not Sephardic like us, or Ashkenazi like others, but Romaniotes. A biblical reference to Rhodes was mentioned in Genesis, something our rabbi pointed out to us about our proud heritage, mentioning Dodanim, Noah's great-grandson, with reverence. The Jews of Rhodes were even mentioned in the Book of Macabees. A kinship to our history and a marriage to an Italian gave me a different perspective.

During this terrible time there was an active resistance movement happening around me. Some Jewish girls of fifteen and older escaped to the interior mountains to plan sabotage. I wish I could have gone with them to make the war end faster. But, with three children I was not portable.

Then it got worse. I made a list of events as I learned about them from the broadcasts that we listened to with slumped shoulders. I wrote them down because we were pawns in events we had no way to control. Each one was a blow of uncertainty.

On July 25, 1943 Mussolini, that terrible dictator, was arrested and martial law ruled Italy. The tension was felt in every home, store and transaction. Chaos was more frightening than "Il Duce," the name he called himself. "The Leader" was a disappointment, though I dared not utter that outside the walls of our home.

The Battle of Rhodes was a prelude for what was to come. The Germans came in with caution at the beginning of 1943 under the guise that they would teach the Italians how to use Flak batteries and be real soldiers. Luigi told me in confidence that they had sent four German experts to coastal fortifications, which he knew meant grave danger for the navy and his compatriots.

"The numbers are small," Luigi reassured me. "Besides, all our ships are ready. We can maneuver with little notice." We were both naive.

On September 3, 1943, Allies landed in Southern Italy. This gave us hope until the Germans took control of Italy. The Italians surrendered to the Allies on September 8. Luigi told me that most of the Italians in his division wanted to fight with the Allies or go home. When the armistice was announced not only were the civilians surprised, but the Italians, our protectors were shocked. We cowered in our homes, praying to the Almighty we would be saved. I knew Luigi must have been frightened too. He was a peaceful, musical soul who adored his family and took risks to visit us when he could.

The German battalions that had arrived the previous April moved to surrounded us. I was afraid to go to the market when so little food was available. The enemy took whatever they could—the best wheat for bread, the ripe oranges for juice, our wine grapes for the next vintage. My mother teased out a few vegetables from the garden for the children. My brothers disappeared into the mountains with the partisans creating damage where they could. They were gone for weeks at a time. I was afraid to pull out the contraband radio.

The Italians on our island surrendered; however, many of the soldiers escaped to the nearby islands of Kos and Leros, a deep water port nearby, with their weapons. About 1500 escaped, but 6500 were missing. We heard ninety Italians were executed. The Germans cruelty was legendary.

Luigi survived and did not desert, but I saw him only when he could escape from the barracks that became his prison. His commanding officer gave him civilian clothes to commute with ease.

He came with terrible news from my brothers after they met in the forest. He came to the back door and had me go to our donkey shed. We sat on bales of hay. "The Italian Acqui division on Cephalonia was massacred by the Germans on September 21st."

I couldn't speak. I remained silent until I repeated, "A massacre on an island near us?" I had visited once with my father when he was delivering a special order before Rosh Hashanah, the New

Year. I remember my fear because the island had frequent tremors and earthquakes, yet I thought it pretty, but not as beautiful as our Rhodes. I was always a loyalist.

"Yes." Luigi's head fell into his hands. When he looked up at me his eyes were floating with tears for his compatriots. "We were 11,000 and the Germans were 2000 soldiers. So much confusion after Mussolini was killed. Our side thought we would be able to leave, return home. Italians aren't fighters. We're lovers. But, the Germans thought we would use our weapons against them. We dug in while our enemies sent for more troops. I would have surrendered like many because more fighting seemed pointless. After all, we had been allies."

"Oh, don't tell me anymore. This kind of war news sends me into a depth of distress. How can I raise children in such a horrible world?"

"But, with the new invasion the battle came to a head with the siege of Argostoli. Our side held out and then gave up. Germans took full control of the island. Those bastards executed everyone, even three hundred officers who surrendered, and occupied every inch of the island. Murdered more than five thousand out of our nine thousand Italian soldiers, people like me, Luna. Just ordinary young men who were called to duty."

I had difficulty comprehending the slaughter of people who were surrendering. "What about the prisoners they captured?"

Luigi's voice broke, "No prisoners. That was the Germans reprisal."

"But why are they so cruel?" I sobbed for the endless war, the human suffering, my children's inability to be free.

101

Luigi wrapped his arms around me, holding me close. "The Germans see Italians as traitors since we're no longer Allies."

I cried louder until he hushed me. "What's the point of going on?" I stared at his worried face with my tear-streaked one.

"I have a plan," he said.

"What kind of a plan?" I wrung a hankie in my hands, my sign of palpable anguish.

"Just let me work out a few things. I will save us. Nothing is going to keep you and my children from living decent lives. Nothing."

Chapter Twenty-Two

August, 1944

The Italians fought valiantly, but to no avail. Italy was lost. We knew of arrests and displacement of Jews all over Greece at the end of 1943 until July of 1944, but we never dreamed the Nazis would come to our paradise in the middle of the ocean. We thought we were safe as a false sense of peace swept our sands.

Still, Luigi, was agitated. The Italian soldiers were prisoners on their base.

One afternoon he showed up in civilian clothes at our back door. "Luna, hurry, you and the children must get ready immediately."

"Why? Where are we going?" My chest pounded with apprehension. *Were we leaving the island?*

"I don't have time to explain. Dress yourself in a Sabbath dress and put on the children's best clothes." He was so serious, so forceful, so determined for me to follow his orders that I did not have time to object. *Was this his plan?* Whatever it was became urgent.

I covered my head with a scarf, put on my favorite flowered dress, rounded up the children who were like recalcitrant goats and pulled clothes on them; their arms and legs shot out of holes with cries of "You're hurting me. I don't want to go someplace. Where are we going?"

I moved with haste as Luigi's toe was tapping.

"What am I supposed to bring? Are we going on a boat?"

"No, we're walking. Please. Hurry." I noticed an edge of nervousness in his voice. He, who was always confident, sure of his stature as an Italian navy man, kept looking around, as though someone was waiting for us to appear.

I had no idea where we were going but he was strong with a serious air about him. In moments we exited through the back door to avoid our questioning neighbors.

"What about Nonna?" I asked, who was asleep when we left. She had aged and had given up in many ways, her head bowed, shuffling between our rooms, sometimes to the market. Since my father's passing her widowhood became her only persona, a slouched black figure with measured steps that assisted when she could, yet remained silent.

Luigi held the hands of Carmelina, Isaac and Joseph while I carried the baby, Benjamin. "She will be fine."

As we hustled along the street, I still had no idea what was happening. Maybe he knew something I didn't because of news at the base.

Moments later, I was inside the chapel of Santa Maria Vittoria staring at Father Carmine in his long black robe. *Was he sad he lost Luigi to the Jews?* His face was reflected in the baptismal font water at the front. We were instructed to stand in a circle. Carmelina fidgeted with the buttons on her pockets. After some Latin incantations I did not understand and some water dripped on our heads, we were all baptized as Catholics. *Was I still a Jew? How would I explain this to my mother? Was this necessary?* I left without acknowledging Father Carmine. Luigi gave him a knowing nod.

Luigi apologized as we walked back to our home for not telling me first because he knew I wouldn't convert voluntarily. "I am consumed with guilt for returning to Catholicism, but it is for our safety. It is something I felt I had to do."

"Why?" I was furious.

"Because I have a plan. We must survive the terror that is unfolding in Europe. It is dangerous to be a Jew."

Luigi shepherded us home and explained to my mother where we had been. She cried. Then I cried. Our world did not make sense anymore.

"Look, we know what is happening to Jews. Converting to Catholicism will save all our lives. We can still be Jews internally. No one can stop you from saying the Shema or lighting candles."

I was skeptical, but he was insistent. So, the children were enrolled in a Catholic Italian school run by the Christian Brothers, the Péres Salisiens. It was better than having the boys tumbling around our small quarters since our schools had been closed.

I was not happy after centuries of following our Sephardic traditions that my children were being inundated with propaganda from the church. Yet, I was relieved they were in school learning something. They experienced some bullying from the Greek teenagers because everyone knew what we had done. Many of our neighbors were in similar situations of desperation so we remained friends with our fellow Jews. It was only because I had married an Italian that we had a plan.

One morning, shortly after "the conversion," my mother did not wake up. I wept for how her life had evolved to hear Germans shouting orders in the street, their knee-high boots a repulsive symbol of authority. I wept because I no longer had parents. And I wept with relief that she was spared the indignities we were experiencing. I would miss her forever.

As the burial society was still functional, her body was washed, her hair combed and her nails cleaned as they wrapped her in a white linen shroud. We buried her outside the walls in our cemetery. She would never have a headstone but I knew where she was next to my poppa's marker. I went as often as I could to set a stone on each of their graves. Their memories would always be a part of me.

Luigi, who had previously been on Leros to assist with building a naval base, had contacts who must have warned him what was coming. In early July of 1944, before we could observe our September holidays—Rosh Hashanah, the New Year of 5705 and Yom Kippur, our Day of Atonement,— my husband smuggled all of us onto the Italian seaplane carrier, the Giuseppe Miraglia, with only what we could carry. I walked away in the middle of the night with all my possessions in one bag. I hid our Sabbath candles and menorah under my clothes. I could not leave them behind. It was a ship filled with disconsolate and defeated Italian prisoners of war.

We were taken to the Italian refugee camp in Aversa, north of Naples. I had never imagined myself a refugee living among hordes of people with unpleasant sanitation issues. I expressed my complaints to Luigi in letters that may or may not have reached him in our chaotic world.

The children ran wild while Benjamin, the youngest stayed close to me in our barracks. Sheets separated us from our neighbors. I spent my time teaching him what he should have been learning in school, reading, math and Ladino. Someone had to remember where we came from all those centuries ago. When he repeated the phrases it gave me hope our rituals and traditions would be practiced in freedom. His sweet voice accompanied the songs I taught him. My mandolin was left behind, but Luigi promised me a new one when the war was over and we began another life. Would it ever end?

After a month, we were transferred to the International Refugee Organization in Bagnoli, south of Naples. It reminded me of my beautiful Rhodes. I returned to my Jewish traditions and worshipped by myself. I never set foot in a church again. Did a baptism under duress like my Inquisition brethren, count?

Chapter Twenty-Three

March, 1945

When the anti-Jewish laws were instituted on September 1, 1938, we were banned from ritual slaughter to make our meat kosher, non-Jewish servants were dismissed and if people had settled in Rhodes after January of 1919, they were forced to leave the island. We were devastated to see families broken apart; our friends that we had worshipped with for years at the Kahal were packed up and gone. Five hundred souls left in the confusion of the moment on ships for Naples, Tangiers and Palestine. They had no idea how lucky they were to be able to save themselves.

When the Nazis arrived on our shores on September 11, 1943 we were shocked. They moved with precision and speed. First, they imprisoned our governor, Inigo Campioni.

My brothers wrote to me that the following summer events happened like rapid gunfire. On July 18, 1944 the President of the Jewish Community was told all men over sixteen had to report to the vacated Italian Air Force base. They were told to bring identity cards and work permits. I learned later my brothers were hiding with the partisans in the mountains. I had not heard from them in weeks. Most of our neighbors thought they were going to be forced into labor camps so they complied to save their families.

On July 19, 1944 all men reported to the Nazi headquarters. It was not as they thought.

On July 20, women joined their husbands and sons unless they wanted to be shot. Jewelry, money and other valuables were collected, their homes plundered.

On July 21, fear and confusion ensued.

On July 22, all the Jewish women and children were also made to stand in lines for hours.

On July 23, three small freight ships sailed with our Jewish community on board, almost two thousand souls, to Kos, a neighboring island. There, the Nazis picked up another one hundred Jews.

After four days near the island Leros without food and water, the ships stopped in Samos and Paraeus.

On July 31, they arrived at the Haidari concentration camp near Athens.

August 3, 1,604 Rhodesli and Kos Jews were put on trains to Auschwitz, my friends among them. I know this from the 151 survivors who returned to Rhodes and told their stories after the war. Yes, a list is inadequate, but I cannot take the stories of the survivors from them. They spoke the horrors with truth. I cannot begin to describe the human misery that will live inside of us for generations. It was the longest journey of the Holocaust. My brethren were the last to be murdered in the ovens of Auschwitz as some concentration camps in Europe were being liberated.

The war was waning and the Germans were losing. *Why did they murder Jews on islands in the middle of the ocean when the war was almost over?* I asked myself this question through tears. *Where does such a deep hatred come from that erases all reason?*

I cannot conceive of this tragedy and the way Luigi's love lifted us to safety. I will always be grateful to the Italians and their mellifluous language for bringing us together. My heart will always be tortured by the faces of neighbors and friends who trusted in the goodness of G-d and disappeared in a column of smoke. My soul was devastated with grief. One does not recover from such tragedies. Yet, I expressed gratitude for the life I have lived, the love I have received, the children I have born and guidance from Hashem.

BOOK TWO

Shabbatai Tzvi

Chapter One

May, 1947

After time in the Aversa transit camp north of Naples in Oespedale barracato, we made our way to our home in the city of Foggia. The war years haunted me, especially the death of my parents. I still had my youngest, Benjamin, to raise. Carmelina, my oldest, married in the church, a strong adherent to the pageantry of the Mass. How could I object when I had married a Catholic too? At least mine became a Jew. She lived nearby, and although I reverted back to my Sephardic heritage, we were very close. Sometimes she stayed while I lit candles on Friday night and said blessings over the bread and wine to acknowledge the miracle that we were still here. I will always owe my husband gratitude for saving all our lives.

After the Nazis evacuated, my brothers, Bohor and Rudolfo, created small businesses with their partisan friends by importing and exporting to the surrounding islands. Some of my father's old accounts worked to restore their business, but many were gone in the smoke of what we now learned was the Holocaust. Even the small community of Kos had not recovered after losing their teachers, seamstresses, doctors and store owners. I tried not to think of the devastation of Rhodes and every person I knew, the grandparents of my friends, Joya and Maria, the neighbors who had known me since I was a baby, my rabbi, my teacher, my spiritual guide. Such a pure soul. *Who could murder him?* If only we could have saved them all in the bosom of the church.

My older boys, Isaac and Joseph, who were now men with ambitions not realized in a country that lost the war, went to America. They packed trunks of textiles extracted from the remnants of design houses in Milan, a rich collection of brocades, silks and merino wool, along with notions we had hidden, like exquisite bone buttons, Alsace lace and leather for jackets and trim.

A connection they made in Italy sent them to New York to an uncle who had a design studio. Rosenfeld Originals manufactured women's dresses. In their letters they shared that they had lofty ideals of making dresses with matching belts, not house dresses, as soon as they improved their English skills enough to do business. Until then, they made sketches and samples. My boys were clever and hard workers. In time they wrote that they had their own shop with dresses on mannequins in a window, Di Liscia Designs. They sent me a black and white photograph of a stunning dress with a floral pattern and since the silk was sheer, a slip was sewn underneath. Beautiful! Women started to wear shirtwaists similar to a man's shirt that buttoned to the hem.

I asked for samples. They didn't send me that dress but three others made from polished cotton with matching linen coats. I was the envy of my neighborhood and some became jealous. So I put one toward the back of my wardrobe and gave the others to Carmelina. She sashayed around looking prosperous while I wore other dresses that were a bit faded from too many washings. Italians were so poor after the war and angry at Il Duce for leading them into desperation that there was no point in creating envy. I still felt as though I belonged on Rhodes, in my paradise. I was not an Italian. For a time, Benjamin and I lived with Carmelina and her husband, Vittorio.

Joseph and Isaac, designers of women's fashions in New York City, sent word they were moving their families and business to Philadelphia. The competition on Orchard Street in New York cramped them. They wanted me to come to visit but I was not ready for anything new. I was still trying to figure out the old. I refused to allow myself to wallow in all I had to be miserable about so I kept my thoughts private. I focused my attention on my youngest son who attended a private Catholic school. I wanted him to fit in with the boys in our neighborhood and learn the confidence one feels in safety.

Luigi sent some money, but it was never enough. He was teaching Italian and French in a rural area two hundred kilometers away, so he appeared on weekends with live chickens in wooden crates, pastries from the bakery and garden vegetables, some of it payment from his student's parents. We ate well, played music and read books from the library, although my knowledge of Italian wasn't stellar. I did do one thing unexpected though. I visited the rabbi in the next town where there was a synagogue. I couldn't attend services on a regular basis so I lit my Shabbat candles at home, waiting for Luigi to come back on Friday nights by bus. Benjamin was excited to see his Papa. He was teaching my little one guitar chords and to lift his voice in song. Some weeks he was a disappointed boy.

Benjamin remembered our Shabbats in Rhodes with family and friends. For a while, we had continued on Friday nights with drawn drapes, the same as our ancestors in Spain. He stood next to me, his blue eyes wide that it was no longer forbidden. No more secrets. He was almost eleven and there would be no bar mitzvah at thirteen. It would be wrenching him away from the only culture he knew. We said the prayers together as I covered my eyes with my hand. I even allowed him to sip the Chianti I used for the blessing, a few moments to express gratitude to G-d that we had survived and pray for those who did not. My spirituality had not left me.

Benjamin asked on a few occasions with the bewilderment of a child, "Are we Jewish or Catholic? Wasn't I baptized in Rhodes?"

I explained that we would never turn our back on our Sephardic heritage after our ancestors were cast out of Spain in 1492. For my relatives the Church had been an oppressor. We were still Jews in our souls. I didn't want to confuse him; however, I could not forget or dismiss my one true faith. What I was doing was what the *conversos* did during that terrible time, pretending to be Catholic while remaining Jewish. That was why my forbearers came to Rhodes,—to escape the edict of the Evil Queen Isabella.

"Am I supposed to do the same?" Benjamin asked.

I paused to think about what I wanted for him. I did not want him to forget where he came from and the tenor of generations before us. I also did not want him to be bullied which was the standard for those students who were a little different. "I would like you to understand your history. You are Jewish because your mother is

Jewish and your father, too. He saved our lives by converting us and fleeing the Nazis."

I could not explain why the Nazis were so obsessed that they had to come to the middle of the ocean and murdered all our relatives, friends and neighbors, all innocents. It is rumored that the Nazis in Athens had the Italian Carabineri compile the list of 1661 names by families. They knew where everyone lived on a small island. "We are the only ones who survived from our street." My heart pained me when I said this. It could not begin to absorb the human misery caused for generations by hatred and anti-Semitism. Those of Turkish descent had a friend in the diplomat, Selahattin Ülkümen, who saved fifty Jews from Rhodes when they proved their background.

Benny shifted from foot to foot, those blue eyes boring through me. "I want to stay Catholic."

My heart skipped a beat. "Will you still light candles and say prayers with me?"

"Oh, mama, I love you. Of course. I remember my vava and how devout she was."

"Benjamin, you are my youngest and so precious to me. Maybe when you're older you'll examine your history."

"I will. I promise, Mama. Honestly, I don't believe all that they're teaching me in catechism. I like Moses and his laws better than Jesus, but I accept that he was a teacher too." And then his eleven-year-old skinny boy arms wrapped around me and we held one another.

Chapter Two

Unfortunately, Vittorio took a dislike to Benjamin and hit him every day. I spoke to Carmelina, but she was afraid of him too. Her devotion was to her three children, my grandchildren, but not to her brother. I do not know why he was filled with anger, perhaps because Italy lost the war. He was a day laborer with two more mouths to feed, but it got to me to see my vulnerable child with bruises. One day I hugged Carmelina and my grandchildren before I took Benjamin's hand and led him to the bus station. Rome was our destination, a big city with more opportunities. Later, I thought that Vittorio was annoyed because my youngest was a beautiful boy with wide blue eyes edged in dark lashes. The beauty of youth grips many with jealousy. His countenance drew stares from girls, mothers and grandmothers like me. Such a sweet nature too. An innocent with a good soul who had his young life interrupted with inexplicable tragedies.

I couldn't stay long in the City of Seven Hills with only a little money from Luigi. I rented a room in a house outside the ghetto from a Catholic family. I did not share my one true faith, even though

Italians were not known for prejudices. Within the oldest Jewish community in the world, the remnants of our people evaporated. I looked into schools, but the tuition was high and Benjamin would still be the new kid. No matter. Settling in to a new life I taught him myself about history with old books I found on a shelf. I learned what happened during the war from my hosts, an elderly couple who doted on Benjamin. We shared their refrigerator for breakfast and used a hot plate in our room to heat soup enhanced with chicken bones and vegetables. A few times we visited a nearby café.

What I wasn't prepared for was the chaos in Rome,—so many refugees begging on the streets, the smell of rotted food in gutters, the rubble of bombed buildings. The Jews of Rome who survived the German occupation in September of 1943, the extorting of gold, the looting of priceless treasures from the libraries, ancient archives and the Rabbinical College, the deportation of over a thousand Jews discovered from door-to-door seizure, who were sent to Auschwitz; and the final indignity of those executed in the catacombs of Fosse Ardeatine. The church, individual priests and nuns did the best they could, but Pope Pius XII failed to condemn what was happening.

Many sought refuge among neighbors and were discovered. Others survived until liberation in June of 1944 by the United States. Jews came out of hiding to celebrate at the ceremony held at Rome's main synagogue. I imagined the greetings, tears and apprehension when finding a friend or relative still alive. All this happened to citizens who could trace their ancestry to the first Jews who inhabited Rome for more than two thousand years, longer than any other city in Europe. No wonder Italians loved the Americans so much!

The streets of Rome remained clogged with beggars in front of churches, skeletal camp survivors, refugees lost without identity papers and Gypsy wagons with children hanging off the sides. Italy chose to become a democratic republic; however, it was plagued with strikes including all the teachers who wanted more pay, a parade of workers machine-gunned in Sicily that caused great unrest, Communist riots and more. This was not the place to raise my last child.

I returned to Foggia in the south with its fertile farming land and rented an apartment near Carmelina. I tried to ignore the unpredictable Vittorio and he did the same with me. I told him in a low voice after a contentious dinner if he ever laid a hand on my Benny again, I would slice him across the neck with my kosher knife while he slept. He knew I kept it sharpened at all times. I doubt he believed me. I could hardly imagine myself doing violence to anyone, but he looked at me as if to say, "You crazy Jewish woman, I don't know what you'll do."

I tended a garden in the backyard with the owner of the building where we lived. Soon I had many of the fruits and vegetables we had grown in Rhodes. Ah, Rhodes, I longed for the island and our previous life every day. In the meantime, Benjamin grew tall and handsome. He was happy to return to his old school, although his math skills had deteriorated.

Chapter Three

November 1947

My life remained simple, a prosaic one with no man around on a regular basis. The women gossiped as to why Luigi was not home every weekend. In my mind his absence was suspicious, but what could I do? At first I stewed about him because I loved him. Jealousy ripped through me. What if there was another? Then, one weekend when he did not appear, Benjamin and I took a bus on the Sabbath, not something I would do since travel is forbidden on our day of rest. I wanted to visit him in his upstairs studio apartment in the village where he taught.

When he first made the arrangements to live there, I assisted with making the small space a home with drapes, a bedspread, new towels, stacked books on shelves and a stocked pantry. He came home almost every weekend because he missed us and my cooking. We had a few glorious reunions. After all, he was still a good-looking man without a fat pasta belly and I still had a head of thick dark hair and an ample bosom. My middle section was plump with childbirths, but I thought of myself as an attractive package, especially in the nighties I sewed myself, a bit low in the front. With the way he hustled Benny to bed so we could be alone, I thought I had a solid hold on him when his hungry body seduced mine. I did find satisfaction. But the joy ended when I took Benjamin to visit that weekend. On the way I shared the story that had been repeated in our family for generations. It was re-told often by my father at holiday dinners.

I wanted Benjamin to know about our Rhodes history and the generations before us. Most came with the Edict of Expulsion and the Inquisition. When they were no longer slaves they escaped to Rhodes with many others to enjoy the beauty of island life with plentiful soil for farming and fish in the sea.

The stories about a Rabbi born in Smyrna who descended from the Jews of Rome, had fascinated me. Supposedly, he could spend days without sleeping. His wild mood swings that he called 'illuminations,' gave voice to his brilliance. Many on Rhodes had spoken about the effect he had on their families, including a scandal he fostered. According to my father, he first appeared in our community as an ascetic from Jerusalem in 1662 on his way to Egypt and the Holy Land. I decided to tell Benjamin the story of his ancestors from the 1660s because they had to make important decisions about their faith. I repeated it as fiction even though it was true.

I liked being a storyteller, which encouraged me to read as many books as I could from a small library or ones that I borrowed from friends. Plus, my imaginative dreams placated me through the night—the wisp of a veil, a sumptuous biblical feast, a brave warrior—romantic notions for a lonely woman.

One day, my father had shown me a letter with flowing Hebrew script that had survived from one of the great-great-great grandfather's daughters from that time. We read it together and I remember most of it because it was shocking. I did not think to bring it to Italy in our rush to safety so it was gone, but I could not forget it. Besides, after so many centuries the edges crumbled in our hands, but the flowing Hebrew script was clear. Perhaps it had been written by a scribe with a case strapped around his waist, the iron gall ink dried in a small glass bottle until water was added.

I took Benjamin's hand in mine. "I have a story for you."

"A true story? Or one you make up to get me to do things I don't want to do?"

"A real story that happened in Rhodes when our family lived in the Juderia in the 1600s. Shabbatai Tzvi was a false messiah."

Benjamin was puzzled. "There was someone who said they were a messiah and they weren't?"

Benjamin and I walked to town, a basket over my arm with goods for my errant husband. I told Benjamin his father couldn't come home so we were going to visit him. I tried not to shop on Saturdays out of respect for Shabbat and my ancestors and of course, in a Catholic country everything was closed on Sundays. Sometimes I went to church with Carmelina and her family so it looked like we fit in, but I thought about other things as the priests strolled the aisles with incense and chanted incomprehensible Latin words

"Yes, it's an important story because it reveals so many lessons."

127

"What kind?"

"The kind that you remember all your life."

"Does it start with 'Once upon a time?"

"It can, but it is still the truth. Our people are great storytellers, especially your grandfather, blessed be his soul."

Benjamin shrugged his shoulders.

"Once upon a time, Rabbi Mosheh de Vushal was our leader in Rhodes. He was from a prominent family, and by the time he was twelve he was being raised by rabbinic scholars in Safed, which was part of Palestine. The city of Safed had trouble and the Jews were being attacked. At the age of twenty-five he came to Rhodes to be a teacher of Torah, our holy book. A busy man, he didn't have time to write out his sermons. He spoke from outlines scribbled on paper. The congregation encouraged him as he shared what we needed to know to repair the world and live meaningful lives of loving kindness.

In the 1600s Shabbatai Tzvi, born on the ninth of Av, a fortuitous day (when the Romans destroyed the Second Temple) in Turkey, promoted the idea that we were entering the Messianic Age. According to the holy books the next Messiah would be born on that day."

Benjamin clutched my elbow. "What does that mean?"

"The Jews have always been waiting for the Messiah to come."

"Why didn't they accept Jesus?"

"Because they didn't feel he was the one." I sighed.

Such a painful history, yet I want this child to think for himself. "Shabbatai was ordained a *chacham* at eighteen, a title that designated him a rabbi. His sermons were devout, except some thought he was disturbed because he would rant and shout. He began to think of himself as the messiah. He had many followers because he seemed able to perform some miracles."

"What kind of miracles?"

"Some were magic; some were with sticks and sleight of hand, like the men with cards at the market."

"Why did they believe him?"

"Because there had been pogroms, a terrible time of destruction of life and property, in the Ukraine in the late 1640s. Three hundred thousand Jews were killed by Cossacks and Tatars. Three hundred Jewish communities were destroyed. People were nervous. Some were hysterical. So when someone showed up who said he could save them, that he was destined to bring all to Israel, the Promised Land, they listened."

"Did your family follow him?"

"No, they didn't, which is why they were ostracized from their community. My father shared he felt wounded when he learned how his family was treated. He even shouted to me because he was so upset, "We are leaders, not followers of false prophets!" But some like Rabbi Hoshea Nantua, who accepted all his prophecies, did. Jews dreamed of being free. It's a cause that drives us because we have been persecuted for believing in one G-d since the beginning of time. Shabbatai Tzvi traveled to many places because Smyrna, his home town, banished him. He searched for more followers to enhance his movement.

So, when Shabbatai Tzvi was on his way to Cairo and Jerusalem, he stopped in Rhodes in 1662. He stayed at Rabbi de Vushal's home where the Rabbi's son, Shelomo, became enamored of him. Shabbatai came to study the Zohar, a treatise of mystical teachings with the Rhodes scholars. He convinced everyone that he would fulfill his mission when he arrived in the Holy Land. He even performed what seemed like the supernatural but others saw as Divine."

"Mama, this is a crazy story. Did Shelomo follow him?"

"Not at first. He was curious because so many devotees were excited by his ascetic presence. He hardly ate. Mostly it was seeds so he became thin but had a rounded beard and a strong mustache. He was supposed to be very handsome."

"What's an ascetic?"

"It means someone who is self-disciplined. They don't indulge in the life around them. Prayer, fasting and abstaining from frivolous activities was the way he was setting an example for others. A serious fellow." I paused to lick my lips. *Was I right to share this history with him?*

"Young women were especially drawn to him. They worshipped him because they could express their spirituality in public. Some became distraught and followed him everywhere in Rhodes. Imagine our byzantine cobblestoned streets with hordes of sobbing women and agitated men who begged to be guided to the Promised Land. Many were delirious when he appeared.

"What does that mean?"

"They lost control and cried for hours. They refused to eat. They had fits over him." Benjamin was quiet and fascinated so I continued.

"One young woman, Ruth, was a devout follower of Shabbatai. She had been promised to Shelomo, the rabbi's son, as was custom, when she was twelve. They kept company with chaperones, of course. But now she was almost ready for marriage." I stopped walking and turned to Benjamin. "Are you sure you want to hear all this?"

"Yes! You can't stop now."

"My father told me a scandal ensued."

"Why?"

"People gave up their peach and sheep farms for a pittance, closed businesses and sold belongings so they could follow Shabbatai Tzvi. Families were torn apart because some wanted to leave and some wanted to stay. Plus, he was married and divorced twice in his twenties because the unions were not consummated."

"What's that?"

"Never mind. I'll tell you when you're older." Benjamin has always been precocious, but I was not going to have that conversation with him. Let his father explain life.

We continued to walk towards the market. "Rabbi Vushal did not approve of Shabbatai's behavior. The followers became restless, gathering in groups, some women with torn clothes and no shoes kept chanting his name. There was chaos in the streets that disrupted our town. With so many opinions and tempestuous women, the rabbi declared that this stranger was a false messiah. Furious, the believers in Rhodes threw rotten fruit at his home. People started sleeping outside in case Shabbatai Tzvi left early. He had arrived with a small entourage, mostly women, who encouraged others to join them on the journey to Jerusalem. Merchants had traveled to other ports; however, few had ever been to the Holy Land. And then it became worse. It shocked the inhabitants of Rhodes."

I stopped at a vegetable stand I frequented to examine olives. The old woman wearing a babushka and widow's clothing knew me but never smiled or greeted me. Her mouth was devoid of teeth. She gave me a mixture in a small bag of Kalamata olives and fat green ones with a pimento inside. I popped one of the black ones in my mouth and offered some to Benny.

He shook his head, no. "Finish the story, Mama."

"The rabbi's son, Shelomo, announced that he and Ruth were going to follow the messiah to Constantinople in three years. Despair ensued with the wails of the family heard in every corridor. His father, our esteemed rabbi, did not approve of Shabbatai or his son leaving, especially with an unmarried young woman. He railed against the false messiah stealing the hearts of the youth from his pulpit. Pandemonium ruled the streets as neighbors and families fought with each other, property was abandoned by the side of the roads and turmoil changed the tone of the synagogue."

"What happened to Shelomo and Ruth?" asked Benjamin.

"First, he claimed that the false messiah told him what would happen in the future, including that he would be named the Messiah in 1666."

"Did people believe him?"

I could tell my youngest son was wrapped up in my tale. But, we were close to the end of the outdoor market and it wasn't a place to discuss such things. Gossip was endless in small towns.

"Wait for our walk home."

I turned to bargain with a vendor about the clean grape leaves stacked in a pile in front of him. I turned them over for inspection. At one time the rabbis told us they weren't kosher because of tiny bugs. I didn't see any. I bought them to wrap my mixture of rice and meat inside with a lemon sauce served on top, one of Benjamin's favorites. I would wrap some for Luigi too.

With my basket filled with eggplants, tomatoes and other vegetables, we began our walk back to our apartment. "Mama, finish the story."

"Be patient, ijo. Shelomo was so in love with Ruth and her passion for Shabbatai Tzvi, that they left in the middle of the night to follow a pilgrimage of people who slipped away on boats for the mainland."

"What? Wasn't his father angry?"

"Furious. But what could he do? He had to attend to the bedlam left behind by his congregation. People wailed to learn their relatives had disappeared in the night, they were lost in confusion, devastated by the abandonment of following the false messiah."

"How did they know he was false? What if he really was the Messiah the Jews had been waiting for?"

Only a child asks those questions.

"Because when Shabbatai Tzvi left for his journey many followed him except for those who thought they would be transported on clouds. He spread convincing fantasies. Of course those prophecies didn't come true." I said the latter with sarcasm to teach Benny not to be too naïve.

"What happened to the people after he left?"

"It was scandalous that a rabbi's son and a young unmarried woman ran off together.

Rabbi Vushal, much to the consternation of the other leaders in town, had to get people calmed down. They decided not to mention Shabbatai Tzvi and erase him from their consciousness." I pause to consider how I would feel if my children ran off to follow a stranger.

After all, Luigi and I were a strong love story who defied my family yet managed to have a happy ending. Love is powerful, whether for Hashem or misplaced into a false messiah, or the attraction of two young people who want to be together.

As we rounded the alley toward our apartment, Benjamin asked, "What happened to Shabbatai Tzvi and the lovers?"

"On the seventeenth of Sivan, which corresponds to the month of May in 1665, Nathan of Gaza, a fervent adherent proclaimed Shabbatai Tzvi the Messiah." I couldn't speak for a moment thinking of my relatives who resisted the pressure to become Sabbateans. *What gave them that strength?*

"By then, the movement had spread to Amsterdam, Venice, Hamburg, Morocco and London. Jews thought he was their savior instead of G-d." I paused to think of our history fraught with stories of betrayal.

We opened the door to our apartment and I prepared the yaprakes.

"Did they get married?" Benjamin asked as he helped me with the mixture that went inside the grape leaves by stirring the bowl.

"In February of 1666, Shabbatai Tzvi and his followers arrived in Constantinople where he was imprisoned under the order of the Grand Vizier. He was moved to several prisons because he kept singing psalms, until he was given a choice by the Sultan Mehmed IV,—a horrific death or converting to Islam."

"Why did they want to kill him?"

"Leaders do not like to be challenged. His supreme influence was a threat to the control that the Sultan had over his people. Don't forget Shabbatai had the ability to convince others he was their savior through tricks, trances and sermons from another world. The Sultan did not want to lose his powers."

"Did he die?" Benjamin asked as he watched me fold miniature pillows of stuffed yaprakes.

"No, he chose Islam, donned a turban and was given a pension for compliance with their traditions."

Benjamin made a grunt, as if he knew that would happen all along. "What about the couple, Ruth and Shelomo?"

"They and three hundred other families converted to Islam with him."

"What? How could that happen?"

"They thought he was still the Messiah. But, when the Ottoman authorities discovered him again singing psalms with the former Jews, he was put in isolation where he died. He was a confused person who made others confused." I swallowed to digest the story. "What did you learn?" I asked him, expecting a childish answer.

"Not to follow false prophets."

Ah, the wisdom of youth.

Chapter Four

March 1948

On that Saturday, Benjamin and I made our way to the studio where Luigi lived during the week, the precious yaprakes tucked into my basket. An unusual warm day blew dust around our shoes turning them from black to white. I knew he would be home or nearby on a Saturday. We would wait for him. Maybe we could recite prayers together, even though I had been lax about attending services. I trudged up the stairs along the side of his building. We waited on the landing. I knocked and then opened the door. No one locked doors in small towns. There was little of value.

One wall served as a kitchen with a sink, stove top with oven underneath and miniature refrigerator with counter space on top. I placed my basket where he would see it. He would be home soon with a wonderful surprise waiting for him.

Unfortunately, I was the one surprised. The front door opened and a woman with uncombed dark hair, holding packages, plunged into the room. She let out a scream.

"Who are you?" she demanded with raised voice.

"I am Luna, Luigi's wife, and this is his son, Benjamin." With hands on my hips, I asked, "Who are you?"

Her expression shifted from anger to shock. She scowled and her mouth fell open.

"Well?" She searched for words, stumbling over a made-up explanation while I watched Benjamin's face become clouded. Poor perplexed kid.

"I am Esther Galante, a war refugee," she said after clearing her throat.

"What are you doing here? How do you know my husband?"

Esther's posture became erect. "He has never mentioned a wife or child," she said, her chin motioning to Benjamin.

"Perhaps not, but we are here for the weekend. What are your plans?"

She looked so insulted I thought she might strike me as we stood squared off at each other. She was olive-skinned as many Italians but her countenance shadowed darker as she raised her voice.

"Luigi and I are friends who . . .,"

Before she could finish, the object of our desire came in with his school bag of papers to grade, even though it was a Saturday. Luigi was the most shocked.

"What is going on?" was all he could utter, glancing between us. He hadn't noticed Benjamin yet.

"Who is this woman?" My voice was not kind. Luigi was at his most awkward, stunned and silent.

"Benjamin, please go downstairs to wait for me," I directed.

Of course, he didn't want to go, but Luigi backed me up and he left slamming the door. His father had not greeted or given him kisses on each cheek as was the custom.

"Do you have an explanation as to what this woman is doing here?" I remained steadfast but I felt an angry pain in my chest.

Luigi walked over to the bed to sit down. His head fell forward into his hands. I turned to Esther. "I think you should leave."

She looked at me as though I had insulted her mother. "Where would I go? I live here."

"Out! Get out now." Enraged, it came out as a bellow from a fog horn at the pier. I pointed my finger toward the door. I wanted to pull her mat of black hair, but I would never win a fight.

Esther gathered a few belongings into a string shopping bag, called Luigi an obscene name in Greek and stomped out the door. I pursued her to the landing to make sure she didn't harass Benjamin who was waiting on the bottom step. He looked up at the racket with a sad expression. She shifted by him and spat on the ground.

"Benjamin, stay there. Don't wander off."

He shrugged his shoulders at me as if to say, "Where would I go?"

I returned to the claustrophobic room, pulled a chair from the table and sat down in front of Luigi, arms folded over my chest, my expression one of disgust. We stared at each other for a good long time. I was afraid to speak because I would start crying.

My emotions got the best of me. "How could you do this to me? Even your son sees you're a philanderer. I'm your wife. I've borne four children with you. Where's your loyalty?" And then I began to sob, large gulps of air piercing my chest.

My head fell forward. He had been my one and only. I cried and cried.

When he reached his arms out to comfort me, I yelled, "Don't touch me! Ever again. Not after you've been with a whore."

Luigi tried to calm me, but I wasn't having any of his weak explanations. "She's not a whore. She survived the camps. Didn't you see numbers on her arm? She's broken."

I did not respond.

In the meekest voice I ever heard, he said, "I'm so lonely here."

I stood. "How long has this been going on?"

"What does it matter?" He shook his head from side to side.

"You are a cheat and a liar! Staying here because you had so many exam papers to read?" Then I used a string of words learned from my older brothers.

"Luna, my Luna, I have never stopped loving you or our family."

"How could you take up with a mistress,—I spit out that word,—and think it wouldn't destroy us? I am going home. Make your choice."

Despite his protestations, I gathered my basket and purse to make a dramatic exit. Benjamin was full of questions as we walked to the bus station. I refused to answer in detail.

"Who was that woman?"

"A friend of your father."

"Why were you yelling and crying, Momma?"

"Never mind."

"Is my father coming to visit us? Will he still teach me guitar? Can I spend a weekend here? I could take the bus myself."

I pressed my lips into a thin line, took his hand and refused to answer. I might start sobbing again as the bile of anger reached the back of my throat. Suddenly, I dropped Benjamin's hand and made my way to scrub bushes on the side of the road, leaning forward to vomit whatever was in my stomach. I reached for a handkerchief to wipe my mouth filled with horrible breath.

"Your Momma doesn't feel well. Let's go to the bus and ride home in quiet."

"Okay," he said with skepticism.

It wasn't the end for Luigi, but it was for me. He had the nerve to show up at our door the next weekend. I was not happy to see him. We fought again, his decision clear. He wanted a wife and a mistress. *Where do men get these ideas?* I still owned my dignity.

It was not the first time I had heard of cheating husbands; however, I would not allow such a thing in my family. I would be strong and fight back.

As my vehement emotions revisited like the tides, I realized that I did not want him to return and resume our lives. I enjoyed my diminutive space with Benjamin, our routine of school, picnics, markets, food preparation and neighbors. Luigi would turn things upside down if he moved in with us. Besides, I would have to compete with Esther.

My body after four children was not something to behold. My insecurities about resuming our conjugal visits where I undressed in the dark and crept to bed in a heavy cotton nightgown were no longer pleasurable. Waning passions made me feel it was duty on both of our parts.

Divorce was out of the question. I had no interest in another man. My decision was one of practicality. As long as Luigi sent money and I could supplement it with my culinary skills, we remained married. In fact, I accepted the situation by no longer calling Esther names. Luigi came to visit Benjamin once a month in the beginning. Later, it became every few months.

Benjamin once asked me, "Did my father leave because of me?"

"Oh, my beautiful boy, no. Never! We live apart because he has a job someplace else."

"Who is Esther?"

Ah, a hard question to answer. "A friend."

142

Time passed. The difficulty of having smart children is the curiosity they exhibit. I told him the truth. After all, he was almost thirteen now, tall for his age with ocean blue eyes and coffee lashes. The girls were already interested and the older boys had taught him the ways of the world.

"Benny," as I called him at home, "Esther is your father's friend. He still loves us, but it's more convenient for him to stay there."

That was all the explanation I felt he needed at the time.

He looked at me so puzzled, I felt concern.

"Was I the fourth baby that destroyed your marriage?"

"Please don't say that. We are still a family. It was the war. No mention of this to our neighbors. I don't like gossip. Promise me."

Benjamin hugged me and we never brought it up again. If Luigi wanted to be a father he had to reach out to Benjamin.

I kept the peace. Luigi worked out of town so people did not know our relationship. Yes, there were a few rumors but they faded away as Benjamin grew up. I considered going back to Rhodes, but it was such a tragedy. Few returned. At first, I stayed inside, sometimes crying into my pillow as soon as Benjamin left for school, contemplating what to do. If I dozed, it was fitful with dreams of a confined space that I could not escape from, a cave with bones scattered around me. It frightened me enough that I forced myself not to stay in bed. I loved the routine of food preparation so I focused my mind on chopping fresh vegetables.

Chapter Five

June, 1950

I examined my options. Divorce remained rare. Of course, I still loved this man whose Romance languages spilled from his lips in song when he strummed the strings of his guitar. Melancholy melodies in minor keys of Sephardic songs did not bring clarity. They made me think of the generations that preceded me, those who fled the Inquisition to settle in Rhodes, and what the future would bring. He could distract me.

Palestine became the state of Israel in May of 1948, and I considered going there to begin anew. But I hesitated to begin again in another country where I had to live on a kibbutz, a communal living arrangement set up for refugees, to work the land. Those who were there expressed gratitude, especially after the British left in early August of 1948.

Some Jews who could not take the hardship of building a new country amidst the hostility of the British and the Arabs, left Israel. How could I take Benjamin with me to such a place? I gave it strong consideration with the idea of going first and leaving him in his father's care, but I dismissed it when the thought of Esther being close to my youngest invaded my thoughts. I would never leave him behind.

A small group of Jews who survived the war, came to my home after I shared my culinary arts. Sweet people whose families had perished, yet they did not know how to heal. Neither did I. Sometimes we just read psalms. One woman, Sarah, who had lost her children, was inconsolable. In fact, her name was Alicia, but she kept the name Sarah that the Nazis forced upon all Jewish women. I prayed she would not take her own life as many survivors contemplated such thoughts. The idea that they were stateless plagued them. She belonged nowhere, so she dreamed of Israel, yet immigration was not allowed. I could not bear the stories of refugees on ships near safe harbors that were turned away. The idea of Jews fighting back and not being led to cattle cars like the proverbial farm animals brought Sarah strength.

Sarah arrived with news one afternoon in the summer of 1946. The war was over, but Nazis wandered the earth in Europe, South America and even the United States of America, where many were allowed in, especially scientists.

"We're taking revenge," she announced in the strongest voice I had ever heard her use.

"Revenge? Against whom?"

"The British who won't give us the land of Israel back."

"What are you talking about?" I could not imagine what had lifted her spirits.

"The Irgun, a group of militant Jews, planted a bomb in the King David Hotel in Jerusalem and killed ninety-one people!"

"What?"

"I am going to help them. I feel a purpose. I'm going to join them."

"But they're not letting anyone in," I tried to reason with her.

"I will get in." And, with that she left and I never heard from her again.

But, a neighbor received a letter from her months later, long after I mourned for the innocent souls killed.

Of course, I was happy for her, that she found a home where she fit in, but it remained a volatile place. At the King David the Irgun had disguised themselves as Arab workers and Sudanese waiters to gain entrance, smuggling the bombs in milk cans. The hotel, built in 1932 as the most modern and luxurious place to stay in Jerusalem, was surrounded with gardens and an olive grove. The Irgun destroyed the headquarters of the British military housed in the southern wing and the nerves of the English with their high-handed ways.

Only six survivors were pulled from the rubble. What was the point of more deaths? Even Winston Churchill criticized the attack. It made me feel worse. It might have been right for Sarah to live among survivors, but it was not something I could fathom. *How I remember the joy of Rhodes!*

I had personal problems to usurp any positive thoughts that drifted my way. I understood men would sometimes stray and women too. Did my mother wonder what my father did on his travels with notions to sell to pretty island women? Perhaps, but women looked the other way to preserve the family. But I did not know how painful it was to be undesired, the lump of misery that seized my soul when I saw a couple tending to each other on the street. I thought we would grow old together. Allowing that dream to fade took time.

When Luigi came to spend time with us, Benjamin was pleased to show him his school projects, invite him to meet his teachers and take walks into the surrounding hills. He could not share my bed; however, I allowed some affection for harmony in our home. Benjamin pretended disgust when we kissed, but I wanted him to see a compatible family. He had asked about Esther, but I told him she helped his dad with the cooking. He was occupied with friends and exploration so it did not come up again until he was older and understood such things. *Well, at least she's Jewish.*

We went on like that for years. Luigi brought money for bills, came home some weekends and made Benjamin fluent in Italian, Greek, Spanish and Ladino. After all, he was still a Jew.

But, we disagreed on many things, including whether Benjamin should have a bar mitzvah, something every male in my family had done except Luigi. He had endured a circumcision for me, a great sacrifice for an adult male; however, he was not thrilled with the idea of Benjamin leaving his private Catholic school to live with the rabbi in the next town in order to learn his Torah portion. Besides, he was fourteen, a bit old for a class of twelve-year-olds.

We fought about it until I gave in. I knew in my soul what my identity was, and, although Benjamin was between two faiths, not unlike the *conversos* who were forced to convert in Spain and Portugal during the 1500s, he knew his heritage too.

It remained confusing to light candles on Friday night repeating blessings over the candles, wine and bread, only to show up at Carmelina's church for a baptism or to light novenas for her ailing in-laws. She, too, still felt the spark of a Jewish soul by saying prayers every day in Hebrew, especially the Shema that declared our belief in one G-d. It was hard to leave behind what had been ingrained in her soul. I adored my grandchildren, all four of them, and wondered what they would learn about their history years from now. Yes, I was their grateful nonna, their vava, who could answer questions about their grandfather when he appeared.

Luigi had chosen Esther. It remained apparent when the portion of his teacher's salary was sent and some was missing. How could I not be resentful? I never wanted another man, yet I wasn't ready to appear in black as so many widows did in Italy after the war. With shoulders curved forward they would gather in groups at the market offering one another consolation for the loss of family and country, a pack of crows brought together by disappointment.

Never fully accepted by my devout neighbors, I kept to myself, baking goods to sell, preparing dishes from my grandmother's recipes with spices: cumin, peppermint, saffron while adding pine nuts and chickpeas, often garnishing with parsley and cilantro. Meat wasn't plentiful, but when I added cinnamon to it, it made people swoon. I also added cardamom to my coffee and rosewater to desserts. Benjamin loved my cooking and told his friends. Eventually I put three tables in our courtyard and some families came to eat what smelled so good. It covered costs with a little extra for Benjamin's tuition.

My older sons, Isaac and Joseph, were in Philadelphia, and had never been back to visit. They spoke English, married women from the Greek Sephardi community, and had children I had never met. So different from Rhodes where we knew everyone. I had regrets about how the war had torn us apart, but no one wanted to talk about that terrible time.

My sons, who were known by a fancy label sewn into dresses, sent a letter on blue onionskin paper inviting me to visit. At first I wrote back it was not possible. Then, Benjamin begged me to take him. He was anxious to see America and all their 1950s cars, the Empire State Building and meet new cousins. His enthusiasm wore me down.

I decided to wait until the end of the school year in 1954 and visit in the summer when Benjamin's school was on hiatus. I had been warned it was hot and humid not unlike Rhodes. As we prepared for our journey, another box arrived with traveling clothes. Jacket, pants, shirts and new shoes for Benjamin and three new dresses and a cloth coat for me. They were smart about sizes, a little large so Benjamin had room to grow when we left in three months. They also sent our tickets for the ship.

One afternoon someone pounded on our door as I was preparing the evening meal to share. I wiped my hands on my apron and opened it.

Melina, the owner of the Greek bakery in town, said, "Hurry. You have a long distance phone call from America. Someone wants to speak to you."

One of my sons, of course. I grabbed a scarf to tie around my head, dropped the apron to the floor and ran after her. As I shuffled behind her in my slippers I worried that it might be bad news. *Why else would someone call?* The expense of a trans-Atlantic call was extravagant! It must mean an emergency. I kicked up dust as Melina raced in front of me. She had left her young daughter in charge of the counter filled with breads and cakes.

Breathless, I charged into the store looking for a black phone.

"In the back," Melina directed me through a curtained doorway.

I approached the table with the receiver left waiting for me. Only a few businesses and the wealthy had telephones. Those who had done well in the black market during the war, had telephones in their homes.

"Hello?"

"Momma, it's Isaac."

"Yes, are you alright?"

"Yes, mama."

"And your brother? The children? Your wives?"

"Mama, we're all fine. I want to talk to you."

"What is it? No one is sick?" I couldn't imagine why he would go to such expense to call.

"Listen, the connection may not hold." Indeed, every third word was eaten by static.

"What is so important to disturb Melina in her bakery to get me?" Impatient with the delay, I urged him to get on with it.

"Momma, listen to me. We want you to come with Benjamin and stay."

Shocked, I tried to digest this strange idea. "Stay? For how long?"

"Forever, Momma. We have big houses and you can stay with us. I promise to make you happy."

I heard a sigh in his voice. "We want to take care of you."

"I can't do that. What about Benjamin and his schooling?"

What a crazy idea! It was not possible. How could I move again, leaving all behind? Besides, Benjamin and I knew no English.

"We have wonderful free schools here. Everything you do in Italy you can do here. Besides, even though you're not divorced, Luigi is no longer your partner."

That stung. I had put up a good front, but it was apparent to everyone, I was no longer Luigi's wife. I did not mourn for him. I had grown to enjoy making my own decisions, being independent, supplementing my meager share of his salary with my culinary skills and sleeping alone. I held no ill feelings toward Esther. Neither was to blame. We were all broken after the Nazis destroyed our lives, especially those who had been in the camps. So few had returned who were not damaged. If they found solace with each other, so be it. Even if Luigi wanted to come back, I wouldn't take him. What for? I no longer desired a man.

"Let me think about this and discuss it with Benjamin."

"Okay, Mama, but I'm only buying one-way tickets."

BOOK THREE

Babatha

Chapter One

September, 1950

Long before Shabbatai Tzvi, another false prophet inspired a following, although this story is fraught with complexity. I had begun to teach what I learned from readings to a group of women from our small synagogue. I wanted them to know how strong the Jews could be under the worst of conditions, especially since many lost so much in the war. I tried out my stories on Benjamin first as he often accompanied me.

We dragged a small wagon pulled by a donkey I had obtained by selling home-made *dolmas* for parties with slices of lemon. The best yaprakes were from the trees in the lower elevations. The mixture of rice, meat and spices with a touch of cinnamon made my mouth water. For every two I tucked into a tray, I ate one.

Most vehicles were requisitioned by the authorities even after the war we all wanted to forget, was over. The poverty was apparent as we passed by hovels on the road with dusty beggars. Luigi came home some weekends from his teaching job and brought fresh vegetables and fruit from the rural area where he lived during the week.

I didn't know what the fascination was with false messiahs. I kept turning over in my mind how so many followed Hitler. *What makes us followers instead of leaders? What gives some the inner strength to resist? To rebel against norms?* That question resonated with me as I shared a story with Benjamin about a woman named Babatha from a town near the shores of Jordan called Maoza. Her image had haunted my dreams. She came to me often now, a woman from ancient times with confidence, and her lover, a warrior. Was she trying to tell me something?

I began as a Sunday school teacher would, explanatory and patient. I had been instructing women for a long time about our history. "The Bar Kokhba Revolt, one of the most destructive events in Jewish history, took place after the destruction of the Second Temple in 70 CE. Shimon Bar Kokhba became the leader of a group of rebels who resisted the Romans. Four hundred thousand of his followers encouraged revolt against the most powerful entity on earth, the Romans, even though the odds were overwhelming."

Benjamin harrumphed in understanding. Sometimes he pretended not to listen as he dragged his toe in the dirt, but I knew better.

"For a time they succeeded, fueling victory after conquest in the Battle of Tel Shalem that cut off the Roman garrisons in Jerusalem. Many thought of him as the messiah, that the winning of so many battles was divinely guided, that the force of G-d was within him to beat such powerful enemies. Some worshipped and prayed for him through all the victories.

The damage the Roman legions exacted on their enemies, the Judeans, did not deter a forceful people. The Emperor Hadrian destroyed any opportunity of reprisal. During 132-135 CE, the Common Era, which meant after the birth of Christ, he found it necessary to bring legions of troops from Britain led by Julius Severus to quell the rebellious spirits of the Judeans. And, fall they did."

"Is this going to be a sad story?" Benjamin asked.

"Yes, unfortunately, we have a sorrowful history, but it teaches you about our strength, our passion for freedom and the love that pushed people to make decisions. It's a true story about another man, a warrior, who some thought was a messiah."

Benjamin plodded along with me as I made my dolmas delivery. I hesitated.

"Go ahead. I'm listening," he tells me with interest. He had always liked my stories.

I continued, "This one is about Palestine before it became Israel, a homeland formed recently where Jews can go. That was not always the case when the world closed its doors to us. Maybe someday we can visit the Land of Milk and Honey.

The people who arrived before and after the war when the British finally let us have our homeland, allowed us to make the desert bloom. Orchards flourish with irrigation. My friend, Sarah, had sent a photo of herself in the market, engulfed among oranges, avocadoes, tomatoes, melons, olives and bananas. I did not recognize her at first because I had never seen her smile. *Should I consider Israel as a home?* Italy had much to offer,—the weather, the food, the culture, but I was not of these people. It was still a Catholic country.

157

I began my story to Benjamin one evening after our meal. We elongated our necks, searching for a cool breeze as we walked off a heavy pasta with a fresh tomato gravy dinner.

We took our donkey for a stroll. "With their thirst for destruction, Dio Cassius, a Roman historian, reported that Hadrian's troops murdered 580,000 Jews, razed to the ground over 900 villages and sacked fifty towns. They were expelled from Judea which was later called Palestina. Most Judeans left for other shores pending certain death, including Babatha, an unusual woman for her time."

I wondered where she found power, her intensity to live, how she could plan an escape and if she and Kokhba were romantic. I abandoned the last girlish notion with a new practicality. They had a strong physical attraction. After all, passion is heightened when lives are threatened. Lust influenced my decision to marry. I couldn't wait for Luigi to bed me.

We had stopped to give the donkey water in a tin dish we carried and sat in the shade of a tree on a bench. I closed my eyes for a few minutes. When I turned to Benny to finish my tale, his steady breaths let me know he had dozed. I did not take it personally. He was a good boy, one caught in the net of his parent's strange marital situation. He was my last. When he left home I would be alone. I appreciated his companionship. He was the end, unless I became close to my grandchildren.

I woke him with a gentle touch and his eyes fluttered open.

"More Babatha?" I asked.

"No, Momma, tomorrow." We returned home in silence as he led the donkey.

That night something strange happened. I settled into my long cotton gown, my hair wrapped in a scarf, sitting on the chair in my room. Babatha's voice came to me after my prayers, in that space of reflective thoughts, whispering as the sail on a boat, puffing and billowing in a breeze. She called me to write down her words. As an obedient student I turned my chair to the table, shivering a bit. With an old notebook that I pulled from a shelf, the back pages empty from my Italian classes long ago, she spoke to me in a clear voice. I wrote what she said. It was as though I was possessed, the image of a woman from ancient times, her hair dressed in pearls, had a message for me. These are her words, not mine.

I am Babatha, the only child of a successful merchant and date orchard farmer born toward the end of the Nabbatean era near the eastern side of the Dead Sea. My two husbands have died, not of my hand, but the forces upon high that can dismiss lives in a blink. I have had to petition the courts to raise my young son, Yeshua, alone and still await their response. I did inherit the expansive date farm that supplies many with work and sweet meats. The locals are not impressed with a mother who has control over her own land and money; however, I am a scrupulous business woman who keeps records to prove my validity. I have no fear of Romans and their violent brutalities; however, I have trepidation with the men who would like to marry me for my wealth or steal my family's legacy. I even issued a legal document that Judah, my second husband, could not make me responsible for his debts. I recorded an official loan to him without interest. Still, his other wife, Miriam, harangues me for money.

We are at war and I feel the strain. I am grateful we have plenty to eat and send pressed fig cakes, fresh dates and dried vegetables to our soldiers. My good deeds have not gone unnoticed. Friends who live nearby have invited me to dinner to meet Bar Kokhba, the warrior who has proved himself many times. I admit I am an admirer of his bravery; however, I am not among those calling him the next messiah. With bronze and silver coins circulating with an inscription of "Shimeon President of Israel" and "Year One of the Redemption of Israel," he is revered by many as a war hero.

Bar Kokhba agreed to a fine dinner as a respite from the battlefield. His reputation preceded him. Tough to the point of cruelty, brave beyond all expectations, brilliant with strategy and inspirational motivation, he has won many battles to become a hero among his peers. They are part of his army; the initiation remains to cut off part of the little finger or uproot a cedar tree clinging to the earth. I have seen these warriors with mutilated hands and it repulses me.

I arrived early to ready myself with my friends, Judith and her husband, Yohanan, an elder statesman of our people who wore a mantle with fringes over his left shoulder. Both my husbands had followed the same custom with gammad, *a design on the bottom of the mantle that resembled the Greek letter gamma.*

When I dressed in my best robes of silken red, ones I did not want to dirty with the detritus of travel, I checked myself in my copper hand mirror. My dark eyes peered out from a pale angular face as I combed my hair and covered it with a gossamer fabric. Before

I exited the room to the courtyard, I used miltos *on my cheeks and lips, a red tint from iron used for many purposes.*

A large man in a soiled tunic sprawled across a chair, head to chest, snoring with a soft rhythm, his legs splayed out in front of him. A cup of wine sat on the floor nearby. I paused to take in the scene, my heart accelerating to a faster beat.

I was repulsed and drawn to him. He was filthy with dirt and blood, matted hair and torn boots. As I stood to take in the vulnerability of a dozing warrior, our host appeared and awakened him with a slap to the shoulder. He jumped to his feet, sword in hand. The two stared at each other until the recognition grew in Bar Kokhba's midnight eyes.

"Aha! You are my hosts!"

"Yes, and you are suffering from battle fatigue!" Then they hugged and laughed.

I disappeared into the shadows to see if I could be of assistance. Our hosts had taken excellent care and soon we were called into a sumptuous feast at a long table, bowls placed at our seats. We sat on benches and passed an array of dates, olives, figs, apricots, eggplants fried in oil, tomatoes cooked into a rich sauce, some small birds that had been grilled on sticks with an abundance of breads and ripe goat cheeses.

I waited until Bar Kokhba took the seat of honor at the top of the table. His hair was washed and combed back so that it touched his shoulders, his body clean from a bath and wearing a fresh tunic with two thick dark stripes called clavi *that revealed his*

161

status. My G-d, he was handsome, even with sun-burned lips. A waft of lemon-scented soap stirred my nose. I chose a place on the bench a few seats away. Our eyes caught and he smiled. I knew the flame of colors I wore would attract him. The encompassing look that swept across my face meant we would become lovers.

That night as the household slumbered, he came to my bed, ravishing me and my hungry body. I had not allowed myself the pleasures of the flesh after burying two men. But it did not mean I was dead inside. We rose and crested with pleasure. He kissed me fully on the mouth and left without us exchanging a word, a piece of skin from his lip on mine. I felt no guilt. I was a woman with needs like a man.

Chapter Two

When the morning light stole inside my shutters, I was afraid to open my eyes. *Was I in my bed at home or in the aftermath of love-making at an estate in Palestine?* Before I raised my eyelids I felt for my nightgown. Instead, my hands touched my bare thighs. In a panic I opened my eyes to find the entire cloth wrapped around my neck. *What had happened?* I pulled the damp gown over my head, flinging a scarf aside too. I was naked, unadorned, while my hands explored my body, gentle fingers giving me chicken bumps.

Benjamin's voice called out, "Mama, will you make breakfast?"

The shock of where I was permeated my being and my head began to pound. My body had been someplace else. It had not been in slumber last night, but searching the Universe to share the story of Babatha, a woman of strength and daring.

"Mama!"

"I'm coming, Benjamin," I slipped a fresh gown and robe onto my shoulders. I picked up the crumpled nightgown on the floor and held it to my face. The breath I took enveloped me with strong perfume, olive oil on slicked hair and the aroma of a man in power.

I went through my day as if wandering inside a cloud, the intensity of my experience shattering what I knew to be real. I would stop, look to the sky and imagine the strength of the warrior, Bar Kokhba, visiting Babatha in her chamber, their bodies illuminated by moonlight. I felt that passion, the letting go of all that mattered into a deep vat of wine, lips sweetened and bruised by the kisses of one who knew how to adore a woman's body. I knew I had not left my bed, yet I felt as though I had journeyed someplace else. I saw Bar Kokhba. I felt Babatha. *How could this be?*

Those thoughts stayed with me all day. Before I lay down that evening, I sat at my desk, afraid of another visitation. The essence of Bar Kokhba seemed real. *Could he be an angel?* Jews believed in angels, but I was a practical woman who never engaged in such thoughts. Yet, I sat at my table, waiting for words to come. When they did not, I put my head on my arms to think. That is where I awoke later, confused with a stiff back and a cramped neck . No one had slept in my bed. I untangled my arms and stared at the notebook pages. Apparently, I had received another visit from the woman who inhabited my soul. I did not know of Babatha until I read my scrawled handwriting leaping across the pages. These are her words:

After a day of inspecting a blight on some of the date palms at the far edge of my property, I spent the next evening ensconced in my own bedroom at home, re-imagining the touch of a man who, without uttering a word, brought me to what I can only describe as ecstasy.

164

While my son slumbered in another room, Bar Kokhba approached me again. I had told my faithful servant, Naomi, I might have a visitor and to admit him. How did I know this? A letter had been delivered earlier in the day. I stroked the seal with the impression of my lover. "Shalom Babatha, I must feel you again tonight, BK." Not see. Feel.

Shimon, the name I used in familiarity, was gentle and vulnerable as we whispered in the dark after our coupling. Yes, I did fear pregnancy, yet I prayed I was past the time for that to happen as I was entering my third decade. We lay in each other's arms, his rough hands stroking, exploring and worshipping my silken body until dawn crept through the shuttered windows. When he stood in front of the light, he reminded me of the gods the Romans and Greeks worshipped, his body an alabaster model for Jupiter. The Romans' pagan leader, Hadrian, wanted to build a palace of worship to Jupiter on the Temple Mount, our sacred space. It made me angry, while his body made me swoon.

My lover appeared for the next two nights and then he vanished. I knew he could not be mine. He belonged to the Jews. "I am here with Divine Spirit guidance to lead our people," he whispered in the dark. His words stayed with me as he swept away in the dawn, the Prince of our people. He took the name Nasi, a Prince.

Shimon Bar Kokhba met cheering crowds wherever he went, a powerful man who commandeered many, performed heroic acts of bravery and inspired others to fight the enemy. A cult of worship bled out around him. Zealots spread ribbons of stories through communities about thousands of Romans killed, those who would make us slaves again, with victory after victory.

Whispers in the market, stories among servants, the elite wondering: Is this the Messiah? Is this the one we have been waiting for? Many of us believed in the mystical reach of Divine Love through this man. The fervor after each victory confirmed what we already knew, what our souls felt: He is The One. We have been waiting for him and the time is now. After all, his name translated to "Son of a star." For those of us who believed in the Goodness, he seemed an angel on earth.

Except it did not happen the way we thought. Battles raged, hundreds of thousands were lost, their bodies left to rot in the sun at the Battle of Bethar because the Romans would not allow us to pick up our martyred for six days. We were frantic. Our laws required immediate burial. What if the rapists of war came where we were?

I directed Naomi and the other servants to pack food into bags made from the soft sleeve of fiber inside the top of palms. They wrapped clear glass bowls the same way, ones I had especially made with etchings so they would not break. I hid some of my valuables in pottery and buried them in the backyard. Finally, I stored all the receipts written on papyri from the sale of my properties that stretched from Petra to Ein Gedi as well as letters of introduction into a leather bag I had fashioned for this purpose. I also had Bar Kokhba's letters, including his orders for battle last year. He entrusted me with them the last time I saw him. Naomi sealed my case with oil to waterproof it, including the long strap that I could sling across my body.

166

I did not know where I was going, but I knew I would need documentation to prove a woman was a landowner. Without my elegant clothes and my hair dressed in pearls, I would not be treated with the respect I deserve. My soul would not allow me to travel with my people and not be of them.

Without warning a courier appeared at our door with a sealed message which he insisted were for my eyes only. I hustled him away after handing him a large bag of dried fruit and a coin with Bar Kokhba's message. I took the letter into my room. Once again, his initials graced the seal.

"Dearest Babatha,

The battles are not going well. Flee now. Go to the caves I told you about near Ein Gadi, close to the Dead Sea. There are two entrances together with a visible column underneath and a dry riverbed below. A difficult climb. Others have taken refuge there in the past. Take your son and household. Wait for me. I will come so we may be together for all time. My heart belongs to you. You give me strength.

Yours,

Shimon Bar Kokhba"

Chapter Three

132 CE

I dreamed of him coming to me in a cave, the stinking smell of war on his skin. "Take leave now," a voice in my head repeated with urgency. Was this how G-d communicated? With messages in your own thoughts? I awoke minutes later with the compelling notion we had to vacate Ein Gedi at once. The breath of night streaked across the sky when I awakened the household to ready themselves. We had to move with haste. Danger drifted close to us.

I filled the last space in my leather pouch with a summons to appear in court to refute a dispute brought by my late husband's wife, Miriam. She seemed to think his property belonged to her. I was not a fool. This other wife laid claim to what was mine. She had annoyed me before with demands. Now I would be unreachable.

In two days, with the light of dawn cresting, we began our journey in the desert to search for an oasis where we could water the animals, rest in the shade of palms and re-adjust our wares. There were twenty-two of us with my maid, Naomi, other servants, farm workers, our close friends, Judith and Yohanan, with whom I dined and met Bar Kokhba and Miriam, the other wife of my husband who irritated me, but was excellent with food preparation. Thank Goodness she was childless, although I invited my servants to bring their progeny so Yeshua would have playmates.

We did not travel far to wait until the heat of the day passed with the sun turning the desert a burning red. I prayed we would not be bothered by man or animal. My prayers were answered when we set out in the late afternoon sun to reach the bottom of the cliffs. The steep wall terrified me. I stood there immobile for a long time while others unloaded wagons of animals, people and goods, to put upon their bodies for an impossible climb. The larger black mouth of the entrances yawned at me with invitation.

One of the men, Saul, who took care of the livestock, climbed toward the entrance with rope tied around his waist. The plan was for him to anchor it to a boulder so we could send up some supplies.

We could not leave the wagons at the bottom for someone to find. Naomi and Jacob, among my most loyal servants, took them apart and stored the wood in bundles to carry. Some they carried on their backs. Saul pulled the other bundles of wood up the side of the mountain until they disappeared, smacking the sides of the monolith. Sapphira, Naomi's daughter, a long-limbed fourteen-year-old, slipped the wheels into crevices at the bottom.

Then we began our trek to safety. David, one of my strongest workers, took the lead guiding us from rock to plateau, all of us hanging by our hands and gripping outcroppings. Some were so narrow I could not grasp them while others crumbled under my touch. Petrified to look down, my hands gripped and loosened as I pulled upward, following those in the lead.

Yeshua was tied with rope around the back of Lazarus, the strongest man. We called to each other. My son was not afraid. An adventure for a child. At first, there was a trail, but it disappeared. Heights made me melt like a candle, my limbs loose and liquid. My heart pounded with the intention of escaping my chest.

As a young girl, on a dare I had donned tunics, wrapping myself below to climb a date palm. When I reached the top, I looked down in triumph and almost lost my grip. I never wanted to do it again. Those who had taunted me to try had to rescue me before I told my father, who would not have approved.

My rope sandals did not hold like toes. I contemplated removing them. My leather bag slowed me down as it shifted on my body. What was so important that I needed to risk myself? The proof of who I was, the owner of four date palm orchards, bills I had paid so my creditors could not accuse me of being a debtor and letters from my lover, some to me but others he sent for safe-keeping. I had everything with me to live a triumphant life with him, the warrior, Shimon Bar Kokhba. Perhaps he was my Messiah, my Prince.

We were almost at the half-way point that was visible from the bottom because a tree grew out of the rock. Yeshua called out and as I turned to look for him, I lost my balance. I hung with one hand to the ledge I had been standing on. My other arm was bound to my body by the leather strap of my case that had fallen off my shoulder.

David called to me, "Wait. I will come to you. Stay where you are."

My heart was beating so fast I only heard thumping, some his words lost in the canyon. I could no longer hold on with my hands. My fingers ached with pain. With the shock of a lightning bolt in a storm, I dropped below, my fall stopped by another ledge. My bag slipped off my arm and sailed below me. I watched it roll down, loosening rocks and small plants. It landed almost half-way down to the bottom against bushes that stopped its wagon-wheel roll.

David called out to me, "Are you injured?"

I did my best to pull to an upright position, but I had landed on my left hip. The pain seared through me, crackling like meat on a fire. I tried again, this time feeling for broken bones.

David called, "Stay there. I will come for you. I will retrieve your bag first."

I lay down on my right side to wait, my hand rubbing the bone of my hip that surely was damaged. I lifted my lengthy tunic to check and saw a purple star spreading across me, but the skin was not torn.

I watched David as he unloaded jugs of water stacked on his back and stored them close to the wall of rock. How would he ever get them back on? He had needed help at the bottom.

I closed my eyes in exhaustion. I was a lady not used to hard labor. My hands did not bear the calluses of servants. I began to doze in exhaustion. As I reached the outer edges of sleep, a wail awakened me. I raised my head to see my rescuer, David, had plunged to his death reaching for my leather bag. His body lay in a pile of rubble as he took a bush, its roots and rocks with him.

Another tragedy. I was helpless. Tears tracked down my cheeks. Have I made a foolish decision to bring others into danger? A brave man, gone.

Am I responsible? Did my own self-importance cause me to flee, especially motivated by a lover? Was this my hubris, that notion of excessive pride instilled by the Greek gods? Would it be my downfall? Icarus, who refused to heed his father, Daedalus' warning, flew from Crete too close to the sun, his wings designed from feathers and wax. He drowned in the sea. The Hellenistic myths were not true, yet their fates wandered in my mind.

We began to shout between those of us trapped in the middle. We called for those below us to reach David. How could we not bury him according to our law? He could not be left for the wild animals, vicious cats, or wolves that ate human beings in a few swallows or vultures that would swirl around him drawing attention to our location. I watched as the others did their best to climb to him, limbs flinging over precipices, a jug lost to the bottom in pieces and the stain of the precious water wasted. I turned to hide my face in my arm and wailed in grief.

David had been my helpmate, among the strongest on the farm. Smarter than most, he sometimes assisted with the financial books and tracking inventory. He taught himself to read and devoured Torah in the evenings. He was also the husband of my devoted Naomi and the father of Sapphira. His three sons were fighting with the army of Bar Kokhba. I felt myself sinking into a devastated state where I considered abandoning this futile journey. Not one to doubt myself after a decision was made, I was filled with questions: What if we all fell off this sheet of rock that looked like it reached the clouds? Who would save me and Yeshua? Would Bar Kokhba find us?

Pain seared through my hip, a lamb sizzling on an open fire for a feast. I could not adjust myself for comfort. With effort, so I would not fall, I stripped my extra tunic off and rolled it to place under my head.

173

Another strong young man, Lazarus, who carried my precious son, placed him on a ledge near others. I saw Yeshua whimpering in fear to have witnessed such a tragedy. I loved this child with all my heart, especially after other pregnancies had not reached full term. I told myself it was G-d's will, but it did not mollify me. Yes, I hovered over him, my precious boy who would inherit my father's pride of four orchards. I would have to make him strong to endure this life.

Lazarus, a man in his late twenties, was comely with broad shoulders. I knew from his gaze he desired me, but I would not allow myself the indulgence of cavorting with a servant, no matter how lonely my bed was at night.

Lazarus reached David and lifted his body up to show me that life was gone, his face tilted away from the sun, eyes open in a shocked stare.

"What should I do with him?" Lazarus shouted.

"Can you carry him to the cave?" I asked.

"Yes, if I carry nothing else."

Lazarus laid the dead man across his shoulders. The weight of David unbalanced him. With an adjustment he hung David's arms around his neck, while his legs dangled down his back. He staggered with the dead weight, and then moved with caution, every step weakened by his load. He veered to the right, away from the path we had taken because there was an outcropping where he could rest. I thought we should all stop until morning. It was not possible for me to put any weight on my leg. I tried. The pain scorched through me. Naomi's echoed wails wounded me.

Then, with bravado, Lazarus left the dead man on the ledge and began a climb down toward my bag! I wanted that bag that had caused so much trouble. It contained the letters of my lover. With the limberness of the young, he reached across to the shelf where it had landed. He stood on the narrow spot, slung it across his body and climbed back to the ledge where he settled in for the night. I, too, dozed off to the sounds of night in the desert—the flapping of bat wings, the singing of the wind, the moans of our people and especially the cries of Naomi who had lost her husband.

Morning brought another tragedy. Lazarus lifted David onto his back, leaving the bag for someone else to reach and bring up. I told myself we would survive this climb. We had to for our people. In a flash as Lazarus turned to ready for the ascent, the weight of the dead man pulled him backwards. Over he went, his long fear-filled howl reverberating through the hills.

He was gone too. I sobbed until I had no tears left. It was my responsibility to lead them to safety. Only G-d could save us now. Two strong men, gone. Grief tore through me. My breaths came as gulps; a fish on the dock, its body flopped from side to side until no more air exploded.

This time we had to leave both behind to the elements, a sin not to bury the dead according to the Laws of Moses. Why had G-d given us no other choices? I directed everyone to stop. We bowed our heads in respect to repeat the words of Kaddish, the prayer for the dead. We returned to our arduous crawl with tears. Now we were twenty. I could not lose another soul. I prayed the Shema, saying the familiar words that guided me.

Saul, the only one of our group to reach the top, was exploring the cave. He appeared in the entrance to tell us of cavernous rooms.

"Are there animals?" I wanted to know.

"No. We will be safe," he replied.

Oddly enough, it was my nemesis, Miriam, who rescued me. I had allowed her to come with us when she showed up at our door while we prepared to leave. I did not like her, but if I turned her away, she would tell others where we had gone so I invited her to join us. Childless, which is why her husband sought another wife, she was a hearty woman with layers of fat from her own cooking. Yet, she was nimble.

Miriam made her way to me, assisted me with standing, my balance to one side, looped my arm through hers. She led me upward to the next ledge while I mumbled complaints about my fate.

Chapter Four

I *limped, as I leaned on Miriam. I could not put weight on my left side. Through the will of G-d we made it below the entrance of the cave while the sun flamed our backs. I saw no possible way for us to reach the yawning mouth where we could hide. What was inside? Saul said there no animals, but were they hiding farther back? Were there dangerous animals? Bears with a ferocious nature were known to sleep in caves. We were staggered across the face of the rocks avoiding deep crevices that could have taken us all. As I strained my neck to look up with my weight on my right leg, I realized there were a few footholds available if someone could climb straight up to a narrow ledge. No tilted angle invited us. How would we enter?*

Sapphira, with thin arms and long legs, called out, "I can do it!"

Her mother, Naomi, in grief, screamed, "Never."

But it was of no matter. They were separated by cliffs and rock faces without any interest in guiding us to safety. A few of the men began to call back and forth as they shifted their bundles. Saul, at the top, encouraged us to wait until tomorrow. The evening would descend in time, plunging us into darkness save the moon.

Matthias, a worker who tended the animals, now carried Yeshua strapped to his front, his boy legs swinging.

He called to Sapphira, "Stay where you are. Do you see a trail to the right?"

Sapphira nodded.

"I will bring you rope to tie around your waist. Are you strong?"

Again, she nodded.

I liked Sapphira because she helped her mother and was like a daughter to me. I gave her hair ornaments and extra treats. If I lost her after David and Lazarus, I would be crushed, unable to continue and face Naomi who whimpered in despair as she moved.

Matthias worked his way over to her. I gasped each time he loosened his hands and feet, reaching toward the next target. He moved closer to Sapphira as she waited on a ledge above me. Would I be able to reach where she was? Ai, poor Yeshua, a boy of six years without a father. I could hear his frightened grunts as we waited.

When Matthias reached Sapphira, I lost his instructions to her in the wind whistling in my ears. I could see she had wrapped rope around her and threw the other end to Saul who caught it.

"The ropes are secure. Send her up," said Saul.

Matthias was pointing in another direction, to a side trail. He began to move and motioned her to follow until they reached a common ledge. There he slipped another stake into the rope around her waist. I prayed it did not weigh this skinny girl down. Darkness slipped over us.

Soon, by the natural light of the moon, a small figure moved upward, hand over hand, her thin legs braced against the limestone, while I repeated the Shema, our daily prayer, the watchwords of our faith, "The Lord is our G-d, the Lord is One." Matthias called out to Sapphira as she moved like a spider reaching for fruit. In time with measured moves, she was next to the cave, but not near enough to enter. How would she reach the opening, especially from the side?

G-d's good grace had her small feet side-stepping on the narrow ledge toward the entrance. Again, I worried about snakes that might be hidden inside our refuge. I kept my fears to myself. Finally, with Saul's guidance she grasped an outcropping of rock and pulled herself into the cave. I was amazed at her feat!

Now Matthias barked out orders again. "Saul, hammer another stake farther into the cave. Tie the rope around it and pull. Does it hold you?"

"Do not worry, my friend. We will all be safe soon."

I forgot about Babatha, and became another widow without the resources to reach my destination. I could not let fear grip me. A vital force surged inside of me to climb a rope into a cavern. I was taught bravery and courage as an only child by my father. My mother always wanted me to be a lady, a woman of the upper classes.

Matthias called out again, "Tie the rope into many knots to hold it, pull on it again and toss the end to me."

179

Sapphira and Saul obeyed and soon rope pooled at his feet. Matthias went first. If it held him, it would be safe for the rest of us. Yeshua let out a yell of joy as he was unwrapped and his feet touched the ground. I breathed a sigh that shuddered from my shoulders to my toes.

So be it. That is how we ascended to the yawning cavern; hand over hand, our feet gripping the wall of granite in front of us as we stretched upward, silhouetted in the moonlight. We grasped each outcropping of rock until our hands burned. The weight of supplies tugged us in another direction, our eyes upward with our feet hunting for the next crevice. Periodically, rocks sheared off and fell making a hollow sound below. That did not deter us. We moved like warriors on a mission. I thought of my lover, his strength, how sweet a reunion would be.

I lay down on my back and cried tears of relief while I cuddled Yeshua and Sapphira. It was the most difficult challenge my body had endured. Naomi came to me with palm oil for my hip and wrapped my hands that had been rubbed raw. I could not complain. David, her husband was gone.

We unpacked some of the bundles with bleached linens, red and yellow wool blankets and coverings made into straw mats for beds. The hard ground of rocks offered little comfort, so we searched for soft depressions of dirt and made our beds there. I found a crevice in a rock that afforded me privacy. It was strange at first to be sleeping among my servants, but that ended with haste. We were all the same now.

The men explored farther into the cave. We shared it with bats and things that crawled but not an angry bear. I found a small split in the rock toward the back and stored my precious leather case there, one that caused the death of my two best men. Now we were twenty.

Chapter Five

135 CE

*W*e *had survived for many months, even with a Roman garrison on the ledge above us. Soldiers waited for a glimpse of someone making their way down to a cleft in the rock with a bubbling spring. The stand-off suited neither of us. They could not reach us without our knowledge in the day light. I had stationed someone near the entrance every night. We expanded into the grotto space that became larger as we explored. Three chambers gave us room to spread out, although part of a ceiling that had crashed before our arrival left boulders in the middle of the first room.*

We had everything we needed except more fresh water. We brought palm branches and citron for Sukkoth, the fall festival of the harvest, although we could not build a wooden sukkah as we use to do outside, so we could dine under the stars.

I shared my space with Yeshua, my brave boy. I had petitioned the courts so I could be his guardian. I would do anything to protect him. Naomi, her daughter, Sapphira and the other women and their children, some of whom had been with me for years and remembered my mother, may her memory be a blessing, and my father. The men and older boys stayed in the back cavern. We shared a common area in the second chamber where we found a damaged hearth from previous inhabitants. We sealed the cracks of the hearth with animal skins, the patches of fur making an odd design. The warmth when we cooked made our hard, cold space comfortable. We could not afford the luxury of burning wood often so I tried to keep a routine as I had at home. I could not examine my orchards, but I could pretend my lover might finish his battles and return to me. I prayed to know he was safe.

Everything I needed was nearby: a sheath of wool for warmth, a polished bronze mirror for my reflection, and my box of cosmetics filled with oils for my dry, desert skin and lips, glass jars with kohl for my eyes, a stone bowl for red rock flakes I used to color my cheeks, a shell from the sea for mixtures with tiny wood spoons, a comb, beads I wove into my hair and my perfume flask, the aroma which had lured my lover into my bed.

Naomi had created a special perfumed mixture for me from myrrh, cinnamon, aloe and the sap from balsam, precious oil cultivated in the Ein Gedi area. What a lovely fragrance! The bush, grown in secret, was so valuable our Jewish soldiers destroyed balsam during the first war to prevent the Romans from taking the precious plants away. I do not know how Naomi negotiated a purchase.

My empty jewelry box remained nearby because I wore my gold earrings and multiple necklaces under my tunic. A jar with wine to help me sleep was nearby. I stretched out on my bed made from woven palm fronds and linens, covered with the same red blanket that I used at home. Yeshua nestled close to me. Our small, private space, unlike the many rooms I came from in Ein Gedi, made me cherish my only son more as he nestled into the crook of my arm.

But, by far, my most valuable possessions were the letters from my lover, Bar Kokhba. I read his missives over and over in the light near the cave entrance. They kept me company while I closed my eyes to re-imagine our coupling, his rough hands on my soft skin, his warrior body on mine, the smell of his hair as it fell forward, our breaths intertwined as we panted to completion. I had never felt that satisfaction with my two husbands. Yet, when would he arrive? What condition would he be in? Maybe he was wounded, or worse. I begged my mind not to go to the place that he might not come to rescue me and all the others. If my thoughts escaped into that dark tunnel, I had to be alone. I turned my back to the others, wrapped myself in the wool blanket and wept in silence.

I was still the boss, so others prepared our meager meals. We made a small oven from soft clay with water on a wall, a trail of tears dripping down to us. With skills I never learned, the others,—I could no longer call them my servants,—ground wheat and made bread for us. Unfortunately, it had small pebbles in it, so our teeth cracked or broke. I shared my two etched plates made from colorless glass I had insisted we bring along with wooden bowls, three knives and keys to my properties. We even brought a sickle in case we could grow crops in the future. Naomi tracked the days on a calendar so we could repeat our prayers over candles, bread and wine on the Sabbath, in addition to those of gratitude that we were still alive.

My friends, Judith and Yohanan, were not used to our circumstances, but they kept their spirits up by assisting the servants with tasks. They also, due to their age, slept for long periods of time. The climb they endured had put them at risk without unspoiled air to breathe in small quarters.

I encouraged them to sit near the smaller cave entrance with me, away from the latrines the men had built. We sat holding our knees, our necks strained to allow clean air into our nostrils.

I was comforted by Numbers, Chapter Twenty, verses seven and eight. They were written on papyrus that I stored in willow baskets. The commandment to Moses and Ahren to speak to the rock for water seemed prophetic to me. We would all survive. My hero would rescue us. I could no longer run, my hip injury leaving me with a sad limp. He would still love me, my essence.

Sapphira, who had become our climber, caught small birds she lured with a few grains and captured on a ledge. We roasted them, saving our two chickens for fresh eggs. Food and firewood became our first chore every morning, as the sunlight announced we had survived another day.

We shared our humble residence with thousands of bats who left their remains everywhere. Many times at midnight they left together, a swarm in search of food. Their wings made the noise of many instruments playing at once without music. The odor of their urine was untenable for me. I put perfume on a square of cloth and held it to my nose when I walked around to make sure my hip did not stiffen. The air was not fresh and Yeshua developed a cough, one that kept us up at night.

Eventually, we ran out of sustenance. The first to die of starvation was a small child of one of the servants. We could not bury him, so I laid him in a leather-lined basket curled the way he was in his mother's stomach, feet to head, wrapped in a linen tunic and covered by a mat. I had to leave it close to the entrance because of the smell. We said prayers and observed the ritual burial laws by sitting in a circle for almost a week. Later, I had him moved to the back where the odor was not so pungent.

We ate salted fish we had brought with us; although it increased our thirst. We also had nuts, dates and figs. I missed tzir, the sauce we made from the scraps of fish that enhanced our meals. Sometimes my mouth filled with water when I thought about the flesh of a lamb I had eaten at Pesach in previous years.

Gathering food was an issue and eventually the chickens became supper, the bones sucked dry, but not before others had passed. The grief we felt coupled with abandonment made us fight among ourselves. Some wanted to leave, but I would not allow it. If the Roman legion above us saw us exiting, we would be taken as slaves. Our people had suffered too long in Egypt resurrecting monuments to pharaohs. I could not let it happen again.

I wait for my lover as close to the entrance as I dare, because our toilets are near the entrance, but bodies pile up. We were twenty, then fifteen, ten, now five. Even my nemesis, Miriam has passed. We dragged the bodies to the farthest chamber in the back, although it is difficult to get to with our uneven floors. I know the identity of each one that stared into our abyss with empty sockets.

In the middle room with a hearth, we prepared food, what little there is of it. Naomi, Sapphira, and my beautiful boy, Yeshua, remained plus Matthias. No arguments over sustenance. There was none. Besides, we were all too weak. Mostly, we slumbered.

I admonished myself for bringing the basket of copper artifacts taken from the pagan temples. They might have some value, but to what purpose? It sat near the entrance, a reminder that more food was a better thought.

Dry jugs of water tilted over our shoulders gave only drops. A waterfall flowed above us with a pool. I heard the drips. It was impossible to reach without being detected by the Romans. Yet, another smaller pool cuts into the limestone and fills up to reveal a spring at the end, one that bubbles with delight. Only Sapphira, my monkey-girl, can reach it, but she cannot carry heavy jugs with water. We sent her back on the treacherous climb with small goat skins to fill. She strapped them to her back. I gave her my sandals because, although damaged by my limp, they were sturdier than hers, yet a bit too large. The extra weight makes her unsteady on the climb. She loses a sandal, yet she accomplishes the task of bringing water to us. Such a brave girl! I measured the water to make sure we all receive equal amounts.

I had nothing to offer, so I isolated myself. I know my fate. If I did not return, my properties would fall into the coffers of the Romans. I reviewed the lists of inventories on papyri, but it was beginning to crumble at my touch. I had heard of another land owner who had his properties listed on a copper scroll that would not disintegrate. I examined the documents in my case, the fifteen deeds, orders I gave to collect wheat and fruit and the letters from Bar Kokhba, my love. Why did G-d allow us to be so close and then pull us apart?

I expected him for months, dreaming sorrowful reunions. Then I leaned against a spot near the back of the first chamber with Yeshua's head on my lap. He sighed with hunger and had not spoken for days. I have endured these risks to save him. We came to the end. Yeshua passed in peace in his mother's arms, my only comfort. No burial, but Naomi, Sapphira and I repeated the Kaddish, the prayer for the dead we have said so many times, recently for Matthias, my loyal servant. I wept in grief for my only child, the pain unbearable.

I vowed to be here until the end, Yeshua's body nearby. I accepted G-d's will, my fate.

Why had I chosen a cave for my last days? I loved Shimon. I had met my match. We understood each other, our power over others and the ability to influence. I wanted to save us and preserve what I had built. Maybe he did think he was the Messiah for brief interludes. Perhaps some even wanted to worship him. In the end, he would not allow it, claiming he was mortal. "After victory," he would say to those who urged him on. It never came. His legacy remained on the gold coins scattered at our feet, President of Israel.

It was difficult for me to pen my last letter, but I had to let Bar Kokhba know I waited, that I had followed his instructions, if he ever came. I gathered my papyrus and a sharp writing instrument. I brought iron-gall ink with me in a small glass jar. It needed to be mixed with tannin from the gallnuts tree that contained copper to make a pigment. Naomi crumbled and crushed the ink with the binder so I could use it, then waited until after I finished, allowing it to dry. I had to be careful not to let the ink pool and ruin the document so, I blotted it with my hem.

"Dear Shimon, my lover, my friend,

On this day in 135 CE I write to tender a good-bye. I treasured our moments together, your bravery and the dreams of victory.

I have missed you in the core of my being. My soul longs for your essence, one of strength and power. Without news I do not know if you are well, wounded or gone from this earth.

Our time together was brief, yet intense. In our first moments, it felt like time wiped away the reality while love erupted as a dream. I would have followed you to Jerusalem and beyond. You commanded my world.

Together we might have led our Jewish compatriots to live in triumph, one of peace with our enemies banished. Instead, it feels like all is lost. Prayers are my only consolation. G-d in his infinite knowledge knows what is best for my aching heart. I thank Hashem for guidance, although my heart aches for the community that has been destroyed, the ashes of our own people scattered across a windy desert. It has been a destruction of biblical proportions without the wisdom of Abraham, the fortitude of Moses and the strength of Esther.

I say goodbye with love in my soul for what might have been.

Yours for eternity,

Babatha

I placed the pen and ink to the side. I was too weak to stand, to check on others, too sad to talk. I was quiet with G-d, a presence who stays next to me for comfort."

Chapter Six

1955, Luna's Epilogue

Finally, I can sleep without my thoughts being inhabited by Babatha. This matriarch kept me awake for nights, a woman who seized power when she could, fierce in her own right and a real leader who inspired me. She gave me strength. She, too, had a broken heart. Perhaps that is why her message resonated with me. I, too, must leave my home. I have everything to live for.

Maybe the romance of a girl starts as fantasy and dissolves into something else. Not more. Not less. I raised four children in a time when the world had gone mad. Luigi saved us, even though he didn't turn out to be the hero of my girlish dreams. He was simply a human with foibles like the rest of us. I will always appreciate him for his foresight, his ability to take the scraps of information that floated as rumors and keep us from harm. Hashem thought it was his purpose. Besides, isn't success measured by how our children learn to be independent from us, kind to others and faithful to G-d?

Finally, I have forgiven Esther, Luigi's companion. How could I harbor hatred when he probably instigated their relationship? So, I wasn't the only woman he flirted with or obsessed over. She had been through a hellish nightmare and behaved as a damaged soul. Perhaps I learned something from Babatha's generosity of spirit, her acceptance of Miriam and her offer to travel with them. It didn't save her, but with marauding armies, who knows if she would have survived outside of the cave for long?

For Benny, my baby, it was the hardest, but he has grown strong in our circumstances. He knows who he is: a Jew with history from Roman times. Our personal narrative never leaves us. It grows and adapts to the modern, all the while keeping the remainders of the past buried deep inside of us.

Yet, when my mind quiets I wonder if Babatha and the zealots of Bar Kokhba will be discovered some day, asleep in their cave, her letters hidden in a leather case, brave souls who refused to be captured by the Romans in wait above them.

It is not unlike those who sacrificed themselves at Masada, a hilltop between Ein Gadi and Sodom, where almost a thousand lived with their families after they sought refuge from the First Jewish Revolt in the Judean desert. They lived and prayed while the Roman garrisons below waited. Finally, with an oncoming onslaught, they took their own lives. Where does such defiance and power come from?

Babatha's story has floated over me like a sheet dried in the wind. Her loss feels like mine, a lover who disappears into battle and does not survive. Mine left me for another woman and it stabs my heart. Perhaps my sons are right. A new life in America might give me another perspective. After all, I am no longer young. My interests in romantic love have waned. I seek peace. Perhaps that is what I'll find living near my two older sons, their wives and six children, whom I barely know. That is my purpose, to be close to those that I love. It will be sad to leave Carmelina; however, she will visit. Besides, she is in the bosom of the church. I pray they do not smother her.

As for Luigi, I have forgiven him. After all, he saved our lives. Otherwise, I would have been pushed on board a ship by Nazis and taken to my death like my neighbors. I will never forget the shock of the truth when so few returned to my island paradise.

The war was a terrible time, but as I watch my Benny blossom in a new environment without the threat of bullies and the fear of evil, I realize we were fortunate. I will always grieve for my friends. Luigi is now living close to Carmelina. Esther, his paramour, had a mental break down as did many others from the camps. I hold no ill feelings. After all, it allowed me to come to the United States, a land of freedom.

In my new home I can still make our traditional Sephardic foods, observe holidays and chant ancient prayers in Ladino. My sons, their wives and my grandchildren revel in the flavors we have carried across oceans. My brothers, Bohor and Rodolfo, told me when I run out of the spices I brought with me from the Mediterranean; they will bring me back to buy more. They prosper with their island trade business. I know it is said in jest; however, part of me will always be in Rhodes.

When my courageous ancestors came to Rhodes in the 1500s, they left behind centuries of culture in Spain and Portugal. What were they thinking when they sailed on ships without the few belongings they were forced to surrender to the Evil Queen Isabella? What had she not confiscated besides their souls? What must my ancestors have thought as they were cast out of so many places and led to crematoriums? Did they ask if they were the Chosen People? Were we chosen to be the martyrs for an imperfect world? My life in Rhodes, then Italy and now America means I learned to be adaptable, to accept the true nature of what is happening and to have gratitude every day. My prayers for peace and freedom were answered. We survived.

Our people have begun again many times. It gives me a potent strength to be welcomed in the land of opportunity. And, to give up wearing black. How can the mother of two dress designers endorse mourning? I am alive! Miracle of miracles! I plan to sashay down the sidewalks of the Italian Market in Philadelphia in crisp new dresses with a shopping bag over my arm, purchasing what I need to prepare the meals we love. No one will decide for me anymore.

Ah, the promise of America.

# # #

Author's Notes

The story of Benjamin was told to me in person by the gentleman himself who was haunted by his Sephardic history, the bravery of his family and the history of Rhodes, his birthplace. Luna, his mother, endured much during her life, yet always exuded hope for better times. To be disappointed in love is not unusual. Ultimately, I wanted to craft a story about strong women.

I was introduced to Benjamin by biblical archaeologist, Professor Richard A. Freund, who also shared the story of Babatha. A renowned biblical archaeologist, he authored the *Secrets of the Cave of Letters* (2004) after he and a team excavated the site. The story of an independent woman in biblical times was an anomaly. It included the era of the Bar Kokhba Revolt, a time of extreme bravery and confidence. That their meeting is my invention is a possibility because Babatha had in her possession his letters and coins.

The sheer face of limestone that reached to the sky with two cavernous openings would have terrified me. The difficulty of a fifty foot climb remains jaw-dropping. Babatha arrived without ladders, pulleys or knowledge of what was inside. The television program, *Nova*, shows Dr. Freund entering the cave, a breath-taking feat with modern conveniences. And, yes, it was filled with bats!

Research was also based on archeologist Yigael Yadin's book, *Bar-Kokhba, The rediscovery of the legendary hero of the last Jewish Revolt against Imperial Rome*, a site he explored in 1960 after Bedouins uncovered it in 1953, a short distance away from where the Dead Sea Scrolls were discovered. It was published in 1971, although the news about the largest archive of letters ever found was known much earlier and reported.

In addition, the photographs of the artifacts inspired me. The deformed sandal that revealed the impression of a limp foot, as well as Babatha's clear etched plates, hand-woven straw baskets filled with copper jugs, beads of carnelian, amethyst, agate, quartz and blue glass, sharpened knives, an iron frying pan, intact papyri, incense carriers, the draw-string red leather pouch, goatskin bags, a decorated hand mirror, make-up and perfume and, finally, the actual gold coins with the profile of Bar Kokhba. And so much more!

Ultimately, Babatha's personality came through the letters she saved, the bills she paid, the deeds to four orchards and keys to properties that revealed a meticulous woman of power, unusual for the time. Religious to a fault, gifted with beauty and brains, she commanded respect.

In my research of Rhodes I learned that Shabbatai Tzvi, a false prophet, visited the island in the 1660s. I was familiar with him and curious about the influence he exerted on populations wherever he traveled, only to disappoint his followers in the end. Why did people believe and sacrifice all to follow him? Why did ordinary people accept Hitler in the twentieth century? Are our needs so great we will follow false prophets? These are questions that have been answered and analyzed over many years.

The research I have conducted to glean details has been satisfying, including an extended stay in Rhodes to visit the Kahal Shalom synagogue and visit the streets where Luna walked. I chose to leave out the discovery of a basket of skulls near the entrance of the cave because its origins are disputed. It would be unusual for Jews to separate the head from the body. It is also thought they may have been left by others since many used the caves for protection.

The Diaspora caused by the Inquisitions in the late sixteenth century flung Sephardim all over the world. It affected their mental health for many generations when they were forcibly converted, lost their dwellings and surrendered family members to terror. Out of that reign came strength for a future of freedom, a liberty unknown to many. Those who survived have never given up.

Rabbi Marc Angel's book, *The Jews of Rhodes, The History of a Sephardic Community* was an excellent source by an esteemed scholar. I have used many sources, including actual testimonies from those whose families hail from Rhodes, which is truly a paradise.

I have been researching the Sephardic culture for many years as I have covered the initial expulsion from Spain and Portugal in the *The Blind Eye—A Sephardic Journey* and *Hidden Ones—A Veil of Memories* about the Inquisition in Mexico and the New World. The story of the Rhodesli Jews impacted me. Greece had one of the highest statistics of Jews murdered during the Holocaust, a tragic eighty-seven percent only topped by Poland at ninety percent where my family perished, as I addressed in *Paper Children—An Immigrant's Legacy*.

Finally, I enjoy writing a book when I am also learning with my readers. I, too, have epiphanies when the scope of history creates a significant awareness of what this means. The length of research involved to craft a story from actual events does not allow for frivolous pursuits. It requires a depth of thought infused with facts and motivation. I felt compelled to share this story of love, the inevitability of death, the birth of a new country after a brutal war and the backdrop of the most beautiful island in the Mediterranean brimming with history.

Acknowledgements

Angele and Benny di Liscia were kind to share the story of Luna. I have changed some details to fit my story. Dr. Richard Freund was my guide. I appreciate Rebecca Stohler's expert editing to give me a more refined manuscript, Ghislain's interior creativity, Deb Vesey's comments and Rachel Dahl's book design. Carmen Cohen keeps an eye on all things Sephardic in Rhodes, including the lovely Kahal Shalom synagogue and gift store, while Isaac Habib's tour of the Jewish quarter bristles with passion. Finally, I express a special thank you to my husband, Skip, who has encouraged me in my pursuit of a story. Writing is a lonely sport.

CPSIA information can be obtained
at www.ICGtesting.com
Printed in the USA
LVHW050009041120
670570LV00003B/145

9 780982 695296